A CATHOLIC MODERNITY?

A CATHOLIC MODERNITY?

*Charles Taylor's Marianist
Award Lecture*

• • •

WITH RESPONSES BY

WILLIAM M. SHEA

ROSEMARY LULING HAUGHTON

GEORGE MARSDEN

JEAN BETHKE ELSHTAIN

Edited and with an Introduction by
JAMES L. HEFT, S.M.

New York   Oxford
Oxford University Press
1999

Oxford University Press

Oxford   New York

Athens   Auckland   Bangkok   Bogotá   Buenos Aires   Calcutta
Cape Town   Chennai   Dar es Salaam   Delhi   Florence   Hong Kong   Istanbul
Karachi   Kuala Lumpur   Madrid   Melbourne   Mexico City   Mumbai
Nairobi   Paris   São Paulo   Singapore   Taipei   Tokyo   Toronto   Warsaw

and associated companies in
Berlin   Ibadan

Copyright © 1999 by Oxford University Press, Inc.

Published by Oxford University Press, Inc.
198 Madison Avenue, New york, New York 10016

Library of Congress Cataloging-in-Publication Data
A Catholic modernity? Charles Taylor's Marianist Award Lecture,
with Responses by William M. Shea, Rosemary Luling Haughton,
George Marsden, and Jean Bethke Elshtain / edited by James L. Heft.
p.   cm.
ISBN 0-19-513161-4
1. Catholic Church—Doctrines.   2. Civilization, Modern.
I. Heft, James.
BX1751.2.C3466   1999
282—DC21   98-54133

3 5 7 9 8 6 4

Printed in the United States of America
on acid-free paper

Contents

Contributors

JEAN BETHKE ELSHTAIN is the Laura Spelman Rockefeller Professor of Social and Political Ethics at the University of Chicago. She is the author of many books, including *Public Man, Private Woman: Women in Social and Political Thought; Meditations on Modern Political Thought; Power Trips and Other Journeys; Women and War; Democracy on Trial; and Augustine and the Limits of Politics.* She is the editor of *The Family in Political Thought*; coauthor of *But Was It Just? Reflections on the Morality of the Persian Gulf War*; editor of *Politics and the Human Body;* and editor of *Just War Theory.* Elshtain is also the author of more than two hundred articles and essays in scholarly journals and journals of civic opinion. In 1996, she was elected a fellow of the American Academy of Arts and Sciences. She also writes a regular column for the *New Republic.*

ROSEMARY LULING HAUGHTON is half British, half American. She was born in England and as a young girl traveled widely throughout Europe. She studied art for a time at the Slade School in London and also in Paris. Her later studies in theology have earned her a high place among modern theologians. In April 1981, Rosemary Luling Haughton and six companions bought Wellspring House and established it as a refuge and place of healing for the homeless. She is the author of more than thirty-five books, including *The Catholic Thing* and her most recent work, *Images for Change: The Transformation of Society.* Currently, she is the associate director of Wellspring House in Massachusetts.

GEORGE MARSDEN has been Francis A. McAnaney Professor of History of the University of Notre Dame since 1992. Before that, he held positions at the Divinity School, Duke University and at Calvin College. His books include *Fundamentalism and American Culture* (1980), *The Soul of the American University* (1994), and *The Outrageous Idea of Christian Scholarship.* He is a member of the Christian Reformed Church.

WILLIAM M. SHEA graduated from Columbia University in 1973 with a dissertation on American naturalist philosophers. He taught at Catholic University of America and the University of South Florida and was chairperson of the department of theological studies at St. Louis University from 1991 to 1997. He was president of the College Theology Society (1984–1986) and a resident fellow of the Woodrow Wilson Center at the Smithsonian (1986–1987). His *Naturalism and the Supernatural* was published by Mercer University Press (1984), and he has edited a collection of papers on fundamentalism, *The Struggle over the Past,* for University Press of America (1994) and *Knowledge and Belief in America: Enlightenment Traditions and Modern Religious Thought* for Cambridge University Press (1995). He is currently working on a book on American Catholicism and evangelicalism and on a collection of essays on Catholic higher education.

JAMES L. HEFT, S.M., a Marianist priest, is the University Professor of Faith and Culture and Chancellor at the University of Dayton. He is the author of *John XXII (1316–1334) and Papal Teaching Authority* (Mellen Press, 1986) and editor of *Faith and the Intellectual Life* (Notre Dame Press, 1996). He is currently working on a book on Catholic higher education and serves as the chair of the Board of Directors of the Association of Catholic Colleges and Universities. He is also leading an effort to establish a national Institute for Advanced Catholic Studies.

CHARLES TAYLOR is a professor of Philosophy at McGill University in Montreal. He has taught at other universities in the United States, Germany, and France and held the Chichele Chair for Social and Political Theory at Oxford from 1976 to 1981.

He is one of the leading theorists of the intellectual movement known as communitarianism and is considered to be among the key thinkers in laying the foundation for communitarian thought. Much of his recent work stakes out what he calls a "middle ground" or an "alternative position" between the extremes in today's political and cultural controversies.

Over the decades, Professor Taylor has been involved in Quebec and Canadian politics. He was a candidate for the Federal Parliament on behalf of the New Democratic party on a number of occasions during the 1960s and also served on the executive committee of the party until 1976. He has been actively engaged on the federalist side in the two referenda on Quebec independence in 1980 and 1995.

A graduate of McGill University, Professor Taylor received his M.A. and D.Phil. from Oxford. He returned to McGill in 1961 to teach philosophy and political science. He is married to Alba Romer, an artist, and has five children.

A CATHOLIC MODERNITY?

Introduction

• • •

JAMES L. HEFT, S.M.

In January of 1996, Charles Taylor, whom Richard Rorty recently numbered "among the dozen most important philosophers writing today, anywhere in the world,"[1] gave a lecture at the University of Dayton entitled "A Catholic Modernity?" The occasion was his reception of the Marianist Award. The Society of Mary, whose members are known as Marianists, is a Catholic religious order founded in Bordeaux, France, in 1817; in 1850, its members founded the University of Dayton. The university annually recognizes prominent Catholic scholars, who are invited to the campus and asked to speak about how their religious faith has affected their scholarship and how their scholarship has affected their religious faith.

A number of these scholars have commented that they had never before been asked to do such a thing but nonetheless welcomed the opportunity. For some, the occasion has provided a chance to look at their professional work and their personal faith from a different angle. Those familiar with Taylor's publications, and with some of the current developments in the Catholic tradition, will be able to see that his Catholicism has been a central, if mostly implicit, element in his philosophical writings. At the beginning of the Marianist Award lecture, he explains that the invitation permits him to raise issues "which have been at the center of my concern for decades." As a philosopher, he has felt it necessary to speak indirectly about the religious dimensions of his intellectual commitment to "try to persuade honest thinkers of any and all metaphysical or theological commitments," but in this lecture he has a chance to "open out" a number of the questions that not only Catholics but also all those trying to be authentic and human face in the modern era.

Taylor's lecture not only raises some questions about modernity and Catholicism, as he modestly put it, but also provides a characteristically thoughtful description and evaluation of immensely complex historical, cultural, and religious developments that span the last several hundred years. Some of what Taylor says in the lecture has been developed at greater length in his magisterial study of the history of philosophy, *Sources of the Self: The Making of the Modern Identity* (Harvard University Press, 1989), and in the more recent and more widely accessible *The Ethics of Authenticity* (Harvard University Press, 1992). For example, at the conclusion of *Sources*, Taylor writes that the dilemma of modernity in the West presents an unacceptable alternative: either a commitment to various traditional religious visions that have provided great spiritual fruit as well as untold human suffering or a commitment to an Enlightenment naturalism, or "exclusive humanism," which suppresses the spiritual dimension. Either of these alternatives, argues Taylor, will simply not do.

> Adopting a stripped-down secular outlook, without any religious dimension or radical hope in history, is not a way of *avoiding* the dilemma, although it may be a good way to live with it. It doesn't avoid it, because this too involves its "mutilation." It involves stifling the response in us to some of the deepest and most powerful spiritual aspiration that humans have conceived. This, too, is a heavy price to pay. (p. 520)

In his "Catholic Modernity?" lecture, Taylor states that one path out of the dilemma is provided by Christian spirituality, described "either as a love/compassion which is unconditional, that is, not based on what you the recipient have made of yourself; or as one based on what you are most profoundly, a being in the image of

God." Moreover, such love is possible only if people open themselves to the love of God, which, Taylor adds, "means in fact, overstepping the limits set in theory by exclusive humanisms."

In the body of his lecture, Taylor touches on the complementarity and identity that are characteristic of authentic community. He recalls the stance of Matteo Ricci, the sixteenth-century Jesuit missionary sent to China. Ricci's approach to evangelization helps us to see our own cultural and religious situation more clearly. Taylor sees that the affirmation of universal human rights and of ordinary human life and the notion of human flourishing—all positive values of modernity rooted historically in Christianity—are reasons for both humility and liberation: humility in that these modern notions would never have taken root had not Christendom as a politically coercive force dissolved and liberation for Catholics who are thereby freed to recognize honestly the Church's mixed record and to draw conclusions for appropriating the tradition for themselves and their own times. Finally, having sketched the extraordinarily demanding ideals of modernity's humanism, including "worldwide movements of sympathy and practical solidarity," Taylor asks how Catholics and other people of good will can live up to these ideals and suggests three sources of motivation.

Taylor's lecture deserves further comment and evaluation. Four distinguished observers of the complex relationship between religion and our own age were invited to respond to Taylor's lecture. The first response, from William M. Shea, professor of theology at St. Louis University and student of American philosophy, fills out the historical background for recent extensive revisioning of Catholicism and highlights the impact of the Second Vatican Council (1962–1965). He singles out five contributions as crucial for our own time. In view of the history of the Catholic Church during the modern period, Shea explains that theology must make two crucial judgments: "modernity has not been all wrong . . . and the Church has not been all right." Shea agrees with Taylor that what is needed is neither a "Catholic modernism," which would be to adapt uncritically to the Enlightenment project, which has both positive and negative characteristics, nor a "modern Catholicism," which would constitute the hegemony of Catholic liberals. Like Taylor, Shea chooses the more demanding path of thoughtful and careful discernment of those elements in modern culture that committed Christians not only can learn from but also may embrace. Shea is also confident that the Catholic Church is today moving in a positive direction.

> If Catholic "supersessionism" (the Christian doctrine that the church supersedes Israel in the history of salvation) could be abandoned and anti-Semitism condemned on theological and doctrinal grounds, if the Pope can pray with Hindus, if Catholic theologians will risk all to rethink the relations between the Church and Judaism, Islam, and other world religions, what closed door cannot be opened?

Shea finds that Catholic colleges and universities, rather than secular universities, now provide the most promising arena for the exploration of the meaning of Catholicism in the modern age. These independent institutions have broken with Christendom and with the "bloody forcing of conscience," for which, he adds, we owe a "vote of thanks to Voltaire." Shea asks three key questions, the answers to which, he believes, will determine in large part whether Catholic universities become places where communities of faith and of intellectuals can continue, after Taylor's example, "evaluating and reconstructing the past, discerning what can be carried on and built upon, what must be reconfigured and what laid aside in the church as well as the culture."

Rosemary Luling Haughton, author of more than thirty-five books, mother of ten children, and currently coordinator of a women's shelter in Gloucester, Massachusetts, found Taylor's lecture so stimulating that she is tempted to write still another book! Instead, she chooses here to focus her response on two concepts that she sees as central to Taylor's lecture: the "gospel ethic" and "transcendence." She sees, as she believes Taylor does, the link between these concepts as the source of the bewilderment that many modern Christians experience. Luling Haughton is especially concerned with the changing experiences that make it very difficult to express those new experiences by simply using older concepts, such as those provided by Enlightenment philosophy or "the curious, puritan fastidiousness of neo-Thomism, neatly crossing the river by stepping on well-balanced stones without noticing the water." She does not assume a clear understanding of what might be meant by the "gospel ethic," nor is she confident that Taylor has advanced his own analysis of the weaknesses of modernity, especially its exclusive humanism, by using the general word *transcendence*, a word that too easily lends itself to false dualisms.

The "Renaissance myth"—that is, the myth of the individual's power to achieve—has not led to justice in our own time explains Luling Haughton. Even those democracies that extend voting privileges to all their citizens have failed to contain "corporate power and the oppression and civil rights abuses to which it leads." At least in the Middle Ages, the jurists could assume that the Church's moral code was universal and that the culture supported the carrying out of that code. The social and moral assumptions of that time have evaporated, continues Luling Haughton. Exactly what the "gospel ethic" might mean in our situation is hard to determine; despite "strongly argued opinions," we are today not really that clear on what the social ethic of Jesus was. We do know that the community at the time of Jesus had a clearer sense of its moral responsibility for its individual members than our society does today. In our own day, the "rights culture" assumes that the needs of individuals can be met by laws "quite apart from the moral responsibility of the local community." Developing her argument along these lines, Luling Haughton concludes that the gospel ethic flourished in a culture very different from our own rights culture. Christendom, which extended from about the eighth to the fifteenth century, supported the gospel ethic and, unfortunately, justified a lot of barbarity. Yet, Christendom defended individuals by promoting a sense of justice, though the Church's performance in this regard was certainly flawed. Today the care of individuals is associated with various forms of charity.

And in the Church today, Luling Haughton sees plenty of "life-affirming" attitudes, such as the rejection of Catholic guilt and gloom about sex, but these attitudes are sometimes carried to an extreme that denies the reality of evil. These conflicting movements in the Church she finds bewildering.

> Modern Catholics (and many other Christians, Jews, and people of other faiths) have tried to capture an integral and non dualistic vision of religion that embraces joy and indeed *fun* but also accepts with enthusiasm necessary discomfort, pain or worse if that is necessary for the sake of justice—which turns out to mean a way of life formed by an awareness of created interdependence.

Given this current situation—a flawed modernity and a confused Christianity—Luling Haughton asks whether it is possible to find a language to express "the longing, the passionate unquenched desire that so many people experience." She concludes that it has to do with "mythmaking," not in a naive sort of way that we might imagine as mass-producing meaningful stories through literary effort but rather in an intelligent way that makes it possible for believers to participate in a process of birthing, not only at the instinctual level but also at a level of understanding of what is happening. She underscores the importance of the Catholic notion of sacrament (expressed so well in the film *Babette's Feast*), the new studies on Jesus, some revivals (with a difference) of old "devotions," the emergence of women's rituals (both fairly orthodox and not so orthodox), and the revived interest in Celtic Christianity, with its uncentralized ecclesial system and its ability to absorb and transform pre-Christian myth and ritual. Luling Haughton believes that, were we to draw on these sources within the Catholic myth, such a view of a Catholic modernity "seems both more difficult and much easier, more central to humanity's future and also a lot more fun."

George Marsden, a Notre Dame historian of American Protestant intellectual life, believes that Taylor's lecture exemplifies what Christian scholars ought to be doing: namely, reflecting on how their faith provides important perspectives on contemporary issues. But rather than use the Riccian approach to modernity, Marsden proposes that modern culture is Christianity's prodigal child. Modernity is not foreign to Christians, as Ricci's China was, because a Christian lineage stands behind the accomplishments of modernity. Modernity needs to be called back home through a repentance, for it is not just non-Christian but, in some respects, also anti-Christian, "with all the bitterness that a broken family relationship can engender." Taylor's analysis would be deepened, adds Marsden, if he said something about sin and rebellion, as well as about cultural differences.

Marsden also encourages Taylor not to shy away from the particularities of Christian doctrine and asks, "Like Ricci dressing as a Confucian scholar, do we always have to dress our views in the terms already acceptable to the contemporary academy?" Marsden points to the example of Alasdair MacIntyre, who as a philosopher has enjoyed a wide hearing, even though he explicitly advocates a

Christian alternative. Marsden admires Taylor's work—particularly this lecture—but wants him to exercise less self-censoring of his religiously informed positions. He even prods Taylor by asking him why he has not done more of this explicitly Christian type of reflection and suggesting that the Marianist Award lecture could supply the concluding chapter of his *Sources*.

Finally, Marsden underscores the importance, much as Shea does, of participating in Christian communities of worship and reflection in order to support and sustain distinctively Christian scholarship. People are converted from one paradigm to another not first by arguments but, citing Thomas Kuhn, by "observing the fruitful problem-solving of another community." In other words, the most profound arguments are provided by example—indeed, by witness. Despite these many suggestions, Marsden applauds Taylor as one of the few major Christian intellectuals who has criticized modern culture in the light of his Christian commitment, even if that commitment has remained, except for this lecture, implicit.

The final commentary, offered by Jean Bethke Elshtain of the University of Chicago, focuses on Taylor's vision for a human community that, in her judgment, happily avoids the extremes of homogeneity and incommensurability. She provides an extended reflection on Augustine's thought on the Trinity, by building on Taylor's affirmation that human beings are made in the image and likeness of God, who, for Christians, is trinitarian. So, Elshtain asks, as so many religious people have asked, what does it mean to be made in the image and likeness of a trinitarian God? She finds that "thinking with and through the Trinity permits us to understand why it is that we are unable to express ourselves transparently and to get others to respond to us completely. It enables us to seek the saving grace of our fellow human beings through the transformative and constitutive force of love, *caritas*". Trinitarian reflection strains language. God's ineffability reminds us that we "cannot pin down all of human reality." Recalling that Augustine once remarked that fellowship with one's dog is easier than fellowship with a human being speaking a foreign language, Elshtain nonetheless continues to affirm that being created in God's image allows humans who speak different languages and live in different cultural worlds to realize that they also have something very profound in common.

Much of Taylor's interpretive work on the history of philosophy uses a method of "retrieval," a sympathetic effort to understand carefully what has been said, and then a discernment, in light of current concerns, of what remains of value and of what might enlarge our understanding of ourselves and our culture. Taylor reads these four responses to his reflections on the possibility for a Catholic modernity in a similar way, pondering what they have observed, freely admitting problems in his own thinking, clarifying some of his original statements, and taking the discussion even further.

He divides his reply into seven parts. In response to Luling Haughton's criticism of his choice of the word *transcendence,* he explains that he wanted to "open out the range of possibilities." He also used the Riccian metaphor for a similar reason: to get a certain distance from the subject, a distance that allows a deeper historical sense and provides a clearer view of multiple insights, none of which needs then to assume "the crushing weight of being *the* right answer." He gently touches on a "nuance of difference" between himself and Luling Haughton concerning just how heroic most Christians can be expected to be.

In response to Elshtain's trinitarian reflections, Taylor proceeds to explain that much of modern philosophy, and certainly Kant, has unfortunately turned "monological"; that is, it takes "very little account of the fact that human beings are plural, and even less of their difference." Here, touching on points raised both by Marsden and Shea, Taylor speaks about friendship and community. In general, Taylor finds that much of modern thought is incapable of grasping those goods that exist only when people come together. The exclusive focus on the individual greatly impoverishes our vision for authentic human flourishing. Perhaps the most radical denial of human community, adds Taylor, can be found in the writings of Michel Foucault, for whom freedom was mainly a negative idea that meant escaping the power of others over you. Unfortunately, much of today's multiculturalism shares in this negative view of freedom and underestimates the possibilities of mutual understanding that respects real differences.

In response to Shea and Marsden, Taylor admits that in today's academy the Christian student and professor must breathe in an "atmosphere of unbelief," a fact about which there is neither sufficient reflection nor surprise. Taylor confesses that he was struck by the fact that so many reviewers of *Sources* were unable to grasp what he meant by "moral sources." He was trying to get at a question that modern moral philosophers, especially utilitarians, constantly miss: "What should we love?" Instead, contemporary moralists focus almost exclusively on what should be done. Taylor argues that issues of moral motivation are just as important and even prior to those of moral rightness.

> But, one wants to protest, don't you see that it also matters whether people can actually bring themselves to do the right thing? But then your interlocutor looks at you blankly and says: of course, but that's not moral philosophy; how people actually get motivated, that's in the domain of psychology, or sociology, or whatever.

In the light of such a disconnection between what ought to be done and how we can find the strength to do it, Taylor calls upon Christian scholars to "change the agenda, open it up." In fact, he believes that it is the most important thing Christian scholars should be about.

Taylor concludes his conversation with his respondents by asking why anger, even righteous anger, is so dangerous for the Christian scholar. The conversation among these Christian thinkers exposes the struggle of Christian intellectuals to grasp their vocation in modern culture. Even more broadly, this conversation pinpoints those aspects of modern culture that need to be challenged if a full sense of human life is to be realized.

I wish to thank first Charles Taylor for his stimulating reflections on the possibilities and challenges inherent in Catholicism's relationship with modern Western culture. I also wish to thank William Shea, Rosemary Luling Haughton, George Marsden and Jean Bethke Elsthain for their equally stimulating responses to Taylor's lecture. Carol Farrell, my assistant, and Richard Drabik, my graduate assistant, each contributed generously to the preparation of the text and the index. Finally, I wish to thank my own university for its persistent efforts to understand the Catholic faith in the midst of the promise and perils of modernity.

Note

1. Adam Begley, "The Mensch of Montreal," *Lingua Franca* (May/June 1993): 39.

I

A Catholic Modernity?

• • •

CHARLES TAYLOR

(The following lecture was given at the University of Dayton on the occasion of the presentation of the Marianist Award to Charles Taylor, January 25, 1996.)

I want to say first how deeply honored I am to have been chosen as this year's recipient of the Marianist Award. I am very grateful to the University of Dayton, not only for their recognition of my work but also for this chance to raise with you today some issues that have been at the center of my concern for decades. They have been reflected in my philosophical work, but not in the same form as I raise them this afternoon, because of the nature of philosophical discourse (as I see it, anyway), which has to try to persuade honest thinkers of any and all metaphysical or theological commitments. I am very glad of the chance to open out with you some of the questions that surround the notion of a Catholic modernity.

I

My title could have been reversed; I could have called this talk "A Modern Catholicism?" But such is the force of this adjective *mod-*

ern in our culture that one might immediately get the sense that the object of my search was a new, better, higher Catholicism, meant to replace all those outmoded varieties that clutter up our past. But to search for this would be to chase a chimera, a monster that cannot exist in the nature of things.

It cannot exist because of what 'catholicism' means, at least to me. So I'll start by saying a word about that. "Go ye and teach all nations." How to understand this injunction? The easy way, the one in which it has all too often been taken, has been to take the global worldview of us who are Christians and strive to make over other nations and cultures to fit it. But this violates one of the basic demands of Catholicism. I want to take the original word *katholou* in two related senses, comprising both universality and wholeness; one might say universality through wholeness.

Redemption happens through Incarnation, the weaving of God's life into human lives, but these human lives are different, plural, irreducible to each other. Redemption-Incarnation brings reconciliation, a kind of oneness. This is the oneness of diverse beings who come to see that they cannot attain wholeness alone, that their complementarity is essential, rather than of beings who come to accept that they are ultimately identical. Or perhaps we might put it: complementarity and identity will both be part of our ultimate oneness. Our great historical temptation has been to forget the complementarity, to go straight for the sameness, making as many people as possible into "good Catholics"—and in the process failing of catholicity: failing of catholicity, because failing wholeness; unity bought at the price of suppressing something of the diversity in the humanity that God created; unity of the part masquerading as the whole. It is universality without wholeness, and so not true Catholicism.

This unity-across-difference, as against unity-through-identity, seems the only possibility for us, not just because of the diversity among humans, starting with the difference between men and women and ramifying outward. It's not just that the human material, with which God's life is to be interwoven, imposes this formula as a kind of second-best solution to sameness. Nor is it just because any unity between humans and God would have to be one across (immense) difference. But it seems that the life of God itself, understood as trinitarian, is already a oneness of this kind. Human diversity is part of the way in which we are made in the image of God.

So a Catholic principle, if I can put it in this perhaps overrigid way, is no widening of the faith without an increase in the variety of devotions and spiritualities and liturgical forms and responses to Incarnation. This is a demand which we in the Catholic Church have often failed to respect but which we have also often tried to live up to; I'm thinking, for instance, of the great Jesuit missions in China and India at the beginning of the modern era.

The advantage for us moderns is that, living in the wake of so many varied forms of Christian life, we have this vast field of spiritualities already there before us with which to compensate for our own narrowness, to remind us of all that we need to complement our own partiality, on our road to wholeness—which is why I'm chary of the possible resonance of "a modern Catholicism," with the potential echoes of triumphalism and self-sufficiency residing in the adjective (added to those which have often enough resided in the noun!).

The point is not to be a "modern Catholic," if by this we (perhaps semiconsciously and surreptitiously) begin to see ourselves as the ultimate "compleat Catholics," summing up and going beyond our less advantaged ancestors[1] (a powerful connotation that hangs over the word *modern* in much contemporary use). Rather, the point is, taking our modern civilization for another of those great cultural forms that have come and gone in human history, to see what it means to be a Christian here, to find our authentic voice in the eventual Catholic chorus, to try to do for our time and place what Matteo Ricci was striving to do four centuries ago in China.

I realize how strange, even outlandish, it seems to take Matteo Ricci and the great Jesuit experiment in China as our model here. It seems impossible to take this kind of stance toward our time, for two opposite reasons. First, we are too close to it. This is still, in many respects, a Christian civilization; at least, it is a society with many churchgoers. How can we start from the outsider's standpoint that was inevitably Ricci's?

But second, immediately after we say this, we are reminded of all those facets of modern thought and culture that strive to define Christian faith as the other, as what needs to be overcome and set firmly in the past, if Enlightenment, liberalism, humanism is to flourish. With this in mind, it's not hard to feel like an outsider. But just for this reason, the Ricci project can seem totally inappropriate. He faced another civilization, one built largely in ignorance of the Judeo-Christian revelation, so the question could arise how to adapt this latter to these new addressees. But to see modernity under its non-Christian aspect is generally to see it as anti-Christian, as deliberately excluding the Christian kerygma. And how can you adapt your message to its negation?

So the Ricci project in relation to our own time looks strange for two seemingly incompatible reasons. On one hand, we feel already at home here, in this civilization which has issued from Christendom, so what do we need to strive further to understand? On the other hand, whatever is foreign to Christianity seems to involve a rejection of it, so how can we envisage accommodating? Put in other terms, the Ricci project involves the difficult task of making new discriminations: what in the culture represents a valid human difference, and what is incompatible with Christian faith? The celebrated debate about the Chinese rites turned on this issue. But it seems that, for modernity, things are already neatly sorted out: whatever is in continuity with our past is legitimate Christian culture, and the novel, secularist twist to things is simply incompatible. No further inquiry seems necessary.

Now I think that this double reaction, which we are easily tempted to go along with, is quite wrong. The view I'd like to defend, if I can put it in a nutshell, is that in modern, secularist culture there are mingled together both authentic developments of the gospel, of an incarnational mode of life, and also a closing off to God that negates the gospel. The notion is that modern culture, in breaking with the structures and beliefs of Christendom, also carried certain facets of Christian life further than they ever were taken or could have been taken within Christendom. In relation to the earlier forms of Christian culture, we have to face the humbling realization that the breakout was a necessary condition of the development.

For instance, modern liberal political culture is characterized by an affirmation of universal human rights—to life, freedom, citizenship, self-realization—which are seen as radically unconditional; that is, they are not dependent on such things as gender, cultural belonging, civilizational development, or religious allegiance, which always limited them in the past. As long as we were living within the terms of Christendom—that is, of a civilization where the structures, institutions, and culture were all supposed to reflect the Christian nature of the society (even in the nondenominational form in which this was understood in the early United States)—we could never have attained this radical unconditionality. It is difficult for a "Christian" society, in this sense, to accept full equality of rights for atheists, for people of a quite alien religion, or for those who violate what seems to be the Christian moral code (e.g., homosexuals).

This is not because having Christian faith as such makes you narrow or intolerant, as many militant unbelievers say. We have our share of bigots and zealots, to be sure, but we are far from alone in this. The record of certain forms of militant atheism in this century is far from reassuring. No, the impossibility I was arguing for doesn't lie in Christian faith itself but in the project of Christendom: the attempt to marry the faith with a form of culture and a mode of society. There is something noble in the attempt; indeed, it is inspired by the very logic of Incarnation I mentioned previously, whereby it strives to be interwoven more and more in human life. But as a project to be realized in history, it is ultimately doomed to frustration and even threatens to turn into its opposite.

That's because human society in history inevitably involves coercion (as political society, at least, but also in other ways); it involves the pressure of conformity; it involves inescapably some confiscation of the highest ideals for narrow interests, and a host of other imperfections. There can never be a total fusion of the faith and any particular society, and the attempt to achieve it is dangerous for the faith. Something of this kind has been recognized from the beginning of Christianity in the distinction between church and state. The various constructions of Christendom since then could be seen unkindly as attempts post-Constantine to bring Christianity closer to other, prevalent forms of religion, where the sacred was bound up with and supported the political order. A lot more can be said for the project of Christendom than this unfavorable judgment allows. Nevertheless, this project at its best sails very close to the wind and is in constant danger of turning into a parodic denial of itself.

Thus, to say that the fullness of rights culture couldn't have come about under Christendom is not to point to a special weakness of Christian faith. Indeed, the attempt to put some secular philosophy in the place of the faith—Jacobinism, Marxism—has scarcely led to better results (in some cases, spectacularly worse). This culture has flourished where the casing of Christendom has been broken open and where no other single philosophy has taken its place, but the public sphere has remained the locus of competing ultimate visions.

I also make no assumption that modern rights culture is perfectly all right as it is. On the contrary, it has lots of problems. I hope to come to some of these later. But for all its drawbacks, it has produced something quite remarkable: the attempt to call political power to book against a yardstick of fundamental human requirements, universally applied. As the present pope has amply testified, it is impossible for the Christian conscience not to be moved by this.

This example illustrates the thesis I'm trying to argue here. Somewhere along the line of the last centuries, the Christian faith was attacked from within Christendom and dethroned. In some cases, it was gradually dethroned without being frontally attacked (largely in Protestant countries); but this displacement also often meant sidelining, rendering the faith irrelevant to great segments of modern life. In other cases, the confrontation was bitter, even violent; the dethroning followed long and vigorous attack (e.g., in France, in Spain, that is, largely in Catholic countries). In neither case is the development particularly comforting for Christian faith. Yet, we have to agree that it was this process that made possible what we now recognize as a great advance in the practical penetration of the gospel in human life.

Where does this leave us? Well, it's a humbling experience, but also a liberating one. The humbling side is that we are reminded by our more aggressive secularist colleagues: "It's lucky that the show is no longer being run by you card-carrying Christians, or we'd be back with the Inquisition." The liberating side comes when we recognize the truth in this (however exaggerated the formulation) and draw the appropriate conclusions. This kind of freedom, so much the fruit of the gospel, we have only when nobody (that is, no particular outlook) is running the show. So a vote of thanks to Voltaire and others for (not necessarily wittingly) showing us this and for allowing us to live the gospel in a purer way, free of that continual and often bloody forcing of conscience which was the sin and blight of all those "Christian" centuries. The gospel was always meant to stand out, unencumbered by arms. We have now been able to return a little closer to this ideal—with a little help from our enemies.

Does acknowledging our debt mean that we have to fall silent? Not at all. This freedom, which is prized by so many different people for different reasons, also has its Christian meaning. It is, for instance, the freedom to come to God on one's own or, otherwise put, moved only by the Holy Spirit, whose barely audible voice will often be heard better when the loudspeakers of armed authority are silent.

That is true, but it may well be that Christians will feel reticent about articulating this meaning, lest they be seen as trying to take over again by giving the (authoritative) meaning. Here they may be doing a disservice to this freedom, and this for a reason they are far from alone in seeing but which they are often more likely to discern than their secularist compatriots.

The very fact that freedom has been well served by a situation in which no view is in charge—that it has therefore gained from the relative weakening of Christianity and from the absence of any other strong, transcendental outlook—can be seen to accredit the view that human life is better off without transcendental vision altogether. The development of modern freedom is then identified with the rise of an exclusive humanism—that is, one based exclusively on a notion of human flourishing, which recognizes no valid aim beyond this. The strong sense that continually arises that there is something more, that human life aims beyond itself, is stamped as an illusion and judged to be a dangerous illusion because the peaceful coexistence of people in freedom has already been identified as the fruit of waning transcendental visions.

To a Christian, this outlook seems stifling. Do we really have to pay this price—a kind of spiritual lobotomy—to enjoy modern freedom? Well, no one can deny that religion generates dangerous passions, but that is far from being the whole story. Exclusive humanism also carries great dangers, which remain very underexplored in modern thought.

II

I want to look at some of these dangers here. In doing so, I will be offering my own interpretation of modern life and sensibilities.

All this is very much open to contestation, but we urgently need new perspectives in this domain—as it were, Ricci readings of modernity.

The first danger that threatens an exclusive humanism, which wipes out the transcendent beyond life, is that it provokes as reaction an immanent negation of life. Let me try to explain this a little better.

I have been speaking of the transcendent as being "beyond life." In doing this, I am trying to get at something that is essential not only in Christianity but also in a number of other faiths—for instance, in Buddhism. A fundamental idea enters these faiths in very different forms, an idea one might try to grasp in the claim that life isn't the whole story.

One way to take this expression is that it means something like: life goes on after death, there is a continuation, our lives don't totally end in our deaths. I don't mean to deny what is affirmed on this reading, but I want to take the expression here in a somewhat different (though undoubtedly related) sense.

What I mean is something more like: the point of things isn't exhausted by life, the fullness of life, even the goodness of life. This is not meant to be just a repudiation of egoism, the idea that the fullness of my life (and perhaps those of people I love) should be my only concern. Let us agree with John Stuart Mill that a full life must involve striving for the benefit of humankind. Then acknowledging the transcendent means seeing a point beyond that.

One form of this is the insight that we can find in suffering and death—not merely negation, the undoing of fullness and life, but also a place to affirm something that matters beyond life, on which life itself originally draws. The last clause seems to bring us back into the focus on life. It may be readily understandable, even within the purview of an exclusive humanism, how one could accept suffering and death in order to give life to others. On a certain view, that, too, has been part of the fullness of life. Acknowledging the transcendent involves something more. What matters beyond life doesn't matter just because it sustains life; otherwise, it wouldn't be "beyond life" in the meaning of the act. (For Christians, God wills human flourishing, but "thy will be done" doesn't reduce to "let human beings flourish.")

This is the way of putting it that goes most against the grain of contemporary Western civilization. There are other ways of framing it. One that goes back to the very beginning of Christianity is a redefinition of the term *life* to incorporate what I'm calling "beyond life": for instance, the New Testament evocations of "eternal life" and John 10:10, "abundant life."

Or we could put it a third way: acknowledging the transcendent means being called to a change of identity. Buddhism gives us an obvious reason to talk this way. The change here is quite radical, from self to "no self" (*anatta*). But Christian faith can be seen in the same terms: as calling for a radical decentering of the self, in relation with God. ("Thy will be done.") In the language of Abbé Henri Bremond in his magnificent study of French seventeenth-century spiritualities,[2] we can speak of "theocentrism." This way of putting it brings out a similar point to my first way, in that most conceptions of a flourishing life assume a stable identity, the self for whom flourishing can be defined.

So acknowledging the transcendent means aiming beyond life or opening yourself to a change in identity. But if you do this, where do you stand in regard to human flourishing? There is much division, confusion, and uncertainty about this. Historic religions have, in fact, combined concern for flourishing and transcendence in their normal practice. It has even been the rule that the supreme achievements of those who went beyond life have served to nourish the fullness of life of those who remain on this side of the barrier. Thus, prayers at the tombs of martyrs brought long life, health, and a whole host of good things for the Christian faithful; something of the same is true for the tombs of certain saints in Muslim lands, and in Theravada Buddhism, for example, the dedication of monks is turned, through blessings, amulets, and the like, to all the ordinary purposes of flourishing among the laity.

Over against this, there have recurrently been reformers in all religions who have considered this symbiotic, complementary relation between renunciation and flourishing to be a travesty. They insist on returning religion to its purity, and posit the goals of renunciation on their own as goals for everyone, disintricated from the pursuit of flourishing. Some are even moved to denigrate the latter pursuit altogether, to declare it unimportant or an obstacle to sanctity.

But this extreme stance runs athwart a very central thrust in some religions. Christianity and Buddhism will be my examples here. Renouncing—aiming beyond life—not only takes you away but also brings you back to flourishing. In Christian terms, if re-nunciation decenters you in relation with God, God's will is that humans flourish, and so you are taken back to an affirmation of this flourishing, which is biblically called agape. In Buddhist terms, Enlightenment doesn't just turn you from the world; it also opens the flood-gates of *metta* (loving kindness) and *karuna* (compassion). There is the Theravada concept of the Paccekabuddha, concerned only for his own salvation, but he is ranked below the highest Buddha, who acts for the liberation of all beings.

Thus, outside the stance that accepts the complementary symbio-sis of renunciation and flourishing, and beyond the stance of purity, there is a third, which I could call the stance of agape/*karuna*.

Enough has been said to bring out the conflict between modern culture and the transcendent. In fact, a powerful constitutive strand of modern Western spirituality is involved in an affirmation of life. It is perhaps evident in the contemporary concern to preserve life, to bring prosperity, and to reduce suffering worldwide, which is, I believe, without precedent in history.

This arises historically out of what I have called elsewhere[3] "the affirmation of ordinary life." What I was trying to gesture at with this term is the cultural revolution of the early modern period, which dethroned the supposedly higher activities of contemplation and the citizen life and put the center of gravity of goodness in or-dinary living, production, and the family. It belongs to this spiritual outlook that our first concern ought to be to increase life, relieve suffering, and foster prosperity. Concern above all for the "good life" smacked of pride, of self-absorption. Beyond that, it was in-herently inegalitarian because the alleged "higher" activities could be carried out only by an elite minority, whereas rightly leading one's ordinary life was open to everyone. This is a moral temper to which it seems obvious that our major concern must be our deal-ings with others, injustice, and benevolence and that these dealings must be on a level of equality.

This affirmation, which constitutes a major component of our modern ethical outlook, was originally inspired by a mode of Chris-tian piety. It exalted practical agape and was polemically directed against the pride, elitism, and, one might say, self-absorption of those who believed in "higher" activities or spiritualities.

Consider the Reformers' attack on the supposedly higher voca-tions of the monastic life. These vocations were meant to mark out elite paths of superior dedication but were, in fact, deviations into pride and self-delusion. The really holy life for the Christian was within ordinary life itself, living in work and household in a Christian and worshipful manner.

There was an earthly—one might say earthy—critique of the allegedly higher here, which was then transposed and used as a secular critique of Christianity and, indeed, religion in general. Something of the same rhetorical stance adopted by Reformers against monks and nuns is taken up by secularists and unbelievers against Christian faith itself. This allegedly scorns the real, sensual, earthly human good for some purely imaginary higher end, the pursuit of which can lead only to the frustration of the real, earthly good and to suffering, mortification, repression, and so on. The motivations of those who espouse this higher path are thus, indeed, suspect. Pride, elitism, and the desire to dominate play a part in this story, too, along with fear and timidity (also present in the earlier Reformers' story, but less prominent).

In this critique, of course, religion is identified with the second, purist stance or else with a combination of this and the first "symbiotic" (usually labeled superstitious) stance. The third, the stance of agape/*karuna,* becomes invisible. That is because a transformed variant of it has, in fact, been assumed by the secularist critic.

Now one mustn't exaggerate. This outlook on religion is far from universal in our society. One might think that this is particularly true in the United States, with the high rates here of religious belief and practice. Yet, I want to claim that this whole way of understanding things has penetrated far more deeply and widely than simply card-carrying, village atheist–style secularists, that it also shapes the outlook of many people who see themselves as believers.

What do I mean by "this way of understanding"? Well, it is a climate of thought, a horizon of assumptions, more than a doctrine. That means that there will be some distortion in my attempt to lay it out in a set of propositions. But I'm going to do that anyway because there is no other way of characterizing it that I know.

Spelled out in propositions, it would read something like this: (1) that for us life, flourishing, and driving back the frontiers of death and suffering are of supreme value; (2) that this wasn't always so; it wasn't so for our ancestors, or for people in other earlier civilizations; (3) that one of the things that stopped it from being so in the past was precisely a sense, inculcated by religion, that there were higher goals; and (4) that we have arrived at (1) by a critique and overcoming of (this kind of) religion.

We live in something analogous to a post-revolutionary climate. Revolutions generate the sense that they have won a great victory and identify the adversary in the previous régime. A post-revolutionary climate is extremely sensitive to anything that smacks of the *ancien régime* and sees backsliding even in relatively innocent concessions to generalized human preferences. Thus, Puritans saw the return of popery in any rituals, and Bolsheviks compulsively addressed people as Comrade, proscribing the ordinary appellation "Mister" and "Miss."

I would argue that a milder but very pervasive version of this kind of climate is widespread in our culture. To speak of aiming beyond life is to appear to undermine the supreme concern with life of our humanitarian, "civilized" world. It is to try to reverse the revolution and bring back the bad old order of priorities, in which life and happiness could be sacrificed on the altars of renunciation. Hence, even believers are often induced to redefine their faith in such a way as not to challenge the primacy of life.

My claim is that this climate, often unaccompanied by any formulated awareness of the underlying reasons, pervades our culture. It emerges, for instance, in the widespread inability to give any human meaning to suffering and death, other than as dangers and enemies to be avoided or combated. This inability is not just the failing of certain individuals; it is entrenched in many of our institutions and practices—for instance, the practice of medicine, which has great trouble understanding its own limits or conceiving of some natural term to human life.[4]

What gets lost, as always, in this post-revolutionary climate is the crucial nuance. Challenging the primacy can mean two things. It can mean trying to displace the saving of life and the avoidance of suffering from their rank as central concerns of policy, or it can mean making the claim, or at least opening the way for the insight, that more than life matters. These two are evidently not the same. It is not even true, as people might plausibly believe, that they are causally linked in the sense that making the second challenge "softens us up" and makes the first challenge easier. Indeed, I want to claim (and did in the concluding chapter of *Sources*) that the reverse is the case: that clinging to the primacy of life in the second (let's call this the "metaphysical") sense is making it harder for us to affirm it wholeheartedly in the first (or practical) sense.

But I don't want to pursue this claim right now. I return to it later. The thesis I'm presenting here is that it is by virtue of its post-revolutionary climate that Western modernity is very inhospitable to the transcendent. This, of course, runs contrary to the mainline Enlightenment story, according to which religion has become less credible, thanks to the advance of science. There is, of course, something in this, but it isn't, in my view, the main story. More, to the extent that it is true—that is, that people interpret science and religion as being at loggerheads—it is often because of an already felt incompatibility at the moral level. It is this deeper level that I have been trying to explore here.

In other words, to oversimplify again, in Western modernity the obstacles to belief are primarily moral and spiritual, rather than epistemic. I am talking about the driving force here, rather than what is said in arguments in justification of unbelief.

III

But I am in danger of wandering from the main line of my argument. I have been painting a portrait of our age in order to be able to suggest that exclusive humanism has provoked, as it were, a revolt from within. Before I do this, let us pause to notice how in the secularist affirmation of ordinary life, just as with the positing of universal and unconditional rights, an undeniable prolongation of the gospel has been perplexingly linked with a denial of transcendence.

We live in an extraordinary moral culture, measured against the norm of human history, in which suffering and death, through famine, flood, earthquake, pestilence, or war, can awaken world-wide movements of sympathy and practical solidarity. Granted, of course, this is made possible by modern media and modes of transportation, not to mention surpluses. These shouldn't blind us to the importance of the cultural-moral change. The same media and means of transport don't awaken the same response everywhere; it is disproportionately strong in ex-Latin Christendom.

Let us grant also the distortions produced by media hype and the media gazer's short attention span, the way dramatic pictures produce the strongest response, often relegating even needier cases to a zone of neglect from which only the cameras of CNN can rescue them. Nevertheless, the phenomenon is remarkable and, for the Christian conscience, inspiring. The age of Hiroshima and Auschwitz has also produced Amnesty International and Médecins sans Frontières.

The Christian roots of all this run deep. There was the extraordinary missionary effort of the Counter Reformation church, taken up later by the Protestant denominations. Then there were the mass-mobilization campaigns of the early nineteenth century: the antislavery movement in England, largely inspired and led by evangelicals; the parallel abolitionist movement in this country, also largely Christian inspired. Then this habit of mobilizing for the redress of injustice and the relief of suffering worldwide becomes part of our political culture. Somewhere along the road, this culture ceases to be simply Christian-inspired—although people of deep Christian faith continue to be important in today's movements. Moreover, it needed this breach with the culture of Christendom, as I argued before in connection with human rights, for the impulse of solidarity to transcend the frontier of Christendom itself.

So we see a phenomenon, of which the Christian conscience cannot but say "flesh of my flesh, and bone of my bone" and which is paradoxically often seen by some of its most dedicated carriers as conditional on a denial of the transcendent. We return again to the point our argument was at some time ago, in which the Christian conscience experiences a mixture of humility and unease: the humility in realizing that the break with Christendom was necessary for this great extension of gospel-inspired actions; the unease in the sense that the denial of transcendence places this action under threat.

This brings us back to the main line of the argument. One such threat is what I am calling the immanent revolt. Of course, this is not something that can be demonstrated beyond doubt to those who don't see it, yet, from another perspective, it is just terribly obvious. I am going to offer a perspectival reading, and in the end we have to ask ourselves which perspective makes the most sense of human life.

Exclusive humanism closes the transcendent window, as though there were nothing beyond—more, as though it weren't a crying need of the human heart to open that window, gaze, and then go beyond; as though feeling this need were the result of a mistake, an erroneous worldview, bad conditioning, or, worse, some pathology. Two radically different perspectives on the human condition: who is right?

Well, who can make more sense of the life all of us are living? If we are right, then human beings have an ineradicable bent to respond to something beyond life. Denying this stifles. But then, even for those who accept the metaphysical primacy of life, this outlook will itself seem imprisoning.

Now there is a feature of modern culture that fits this perspective. This is the revolt from within unbelief, as it were, against the primacy of life—not now in the name of something beyond but really more just from a sense of being confined, diminished by the acknowledgment of this primacy. This has been an important stream in our culture, something woven into the inspiration of poets and writers—for example, Baudelaire (but was he entirely an unbeliever?) and Mallarmé. The most influential proponent of this kind of view is undoubtedly Nietzsche, and it is significant that the most important antihumanist thinkers of our time—for example, Foucault, Derrida, behind them, Bataille—all draw heavily on Nietzsche.

Nietzsche, of course, rebelled against the idea that our highest goal is to preserve and increase life, to prevent suffering. He rejects this both metaphysically and practically. He rejects the egalitarianism underlying this whole affirmation of ordinary life. But his rebellion is, in a sense, also internal. Life itself can push to cruelty, to domination, to exclusion, and, indeed, does so in its moments of most exuberant affirmation.

So this move remains within the modern affirmation of life, in a sense. There is nothing higher than the movement of life itself (the Will to Power). But it chafes at the benevolence, the universalism, the harmony, the order. It wants to rehabilitate destruction and chaos, the infliction of suffering and exploitation, as part of the life to be affirmed. Life properly understood also affirms death and destruction. To pretend otherwise is to try to restrict it, tame it, hem it in, deprive it of its highest manifestations, which are precisely what makes it something you can say yes to.

A religion of life that would proscribe death dealing, the infliction of suffering, is confining and demeaning. Nietzsche thinks of himself as having taken up some of the legacy of pre-Platonic and pre-Christian warrior ethics and their exaltation of courage, greatness, elite excellence. Modern life-affirming humanism breeds pusillanimity. This accusation frequently occurs in the culture of counter Enlightenment.

Of course, one of the fruits of this counterculture was Fascism—to which Nietzsche's influence was not entirely foreign, however true and valid is Walter Kaufman's refutation of the simple myth of Nietzsche as a proto-Nazi. But in spite of this, the fascination with death and violence recurs, for example, in the interest in Bataille, shared by Derrida and Foucault. James Miller's book on Foucault shows the depths of this rebellion against "humanism" as a stifling, confining space one has to break out of.[5]

My point here is not to score off neo-Nietzscheanism as some kind of antechamber to Fascism. A secular humanist might want to do this, but my perspective is rather different. I see these connections as another manifestation of our (human) inability to be content simply with an affirmation of life.

The Nietzschean understanding of enhanced life, which can fully affirm itself, also in a sense takes us beyond life, and in this it is analogous with other, religious notions of enhanced life (like the New Testament's "eternal life"). But it takes us beyond by incorporating a fascination with the negation of life, with death and suffering. It doesn't acknowledge some supreme good beyond life and, in that sense, sees itself rightly as utterly antithetical to religion.

I am tempted to speculate further and suggest that the perennial human susceptibility to be fascinated by death and violence is at base a manifestation of our nature as *homo religiosus.* From the point of view of someone who acknowledges transcendence, it is one of the places this aspiration beyond most easily goes when it fails to take us there. This doesn't mean that religion and violence are simply alternatives. To the contrary, it has meant that most historical religion has been deeply intricated with violence, from human sacrifice to intercommunal massacres. Most historical religion remains only very imperfectly oriented to the beyond. The religious affinities of the cult of violence in its different forms are indeed palpable.

What it might mean, however, is that the only way to escape fully the draw toward violence lies somewhere in the turn to transcendence—that is, through the full-hearted love of some good beyond life. A thesis of this kind has been put forward by René Girard, for whose work I have a great deal of sympathy, although I don't agree on the centrality he gives to the scapegoat phenomenon.[6]

On the perspective I'm developing here, no position can be set aside as simply devoid of insight. We could think of modern culture as the scene of a three-cornered, perhaps ultimately a four-cornered, battle. There are secular humanists, there are neo-Nietzscheans, and there are those who acknowledge some good beyond life. Any pair can gang up against the third on some important issue. Neo-Nietzscheans and secular humanists together condemn religion and reject any good beyond life. But neo-Nietzscheans and acknowledgers of transcendence are together in their absence of surprise at the continued disappointments of secular humanism, and together also in the sense that its vision of life lacks a dimension. In a third lineup, secular humanists and believers come together in defending an idea of the human good against the antihumanism of Nietzsche's heirs.

A fourth party can be introduced to this field if we take account of the fact that the acknowledgers of transcendence are divided. Some think that the whole move to secular humanism was just a mistake, which needs to be undone. We need to return to an earlier view of things. Others, among which I place myself, think that the practical primacy of life has been a great gain for humankind and that there is some truth in the "revolutionary" story: this gain was, in fact, unlikely to come about without some breach with established religion. (We might even be tempted to say that modern unbelief is providential, but that might be too provocative a way of putting it.) But we nevertheless think that the metaphysical primacy of life is wrong and stifling and that its continued dominance puts in danger the practical primacy.

I have rather complicated the scene in the last paragraphs. Nevertheless, the simple lines sketched earlier still stand out, I believe. Both secular humanists and antihumanists concur in the revolutionary story; that is, they see us as having been liberated from the illusion of a good beyond life and thus enabled to affirm ourselves. This may take the form of an Enlightenment endorsement of benevolence and justice, or it may be the charter for the full affirmation of the will to power—or "the free play of the signifier," the aesthetics of the self, or whatever the current version is. But it remains within the same post-revolutionary climate.

For those fully within this climate, transcendence becomes all but invisible.

IV

The previous picture of modern culture, seen from one perspective, suggests a way in which the denial of transcendence can put in danger the most valuable gains of modernity, here the primacy of rights and the affirmation of life. This is, I repeat, one perspective among others; the issue is whether it makes more sense of what has been happening over the last two centuries than that of an exclusive, secular humanism. It seems very much to me that it does so.

I now want to take up this danger from another angle. I spoke before about an immanent revolt against the affirmation of life. Nietzsche has become an important figure in the articulation of this, a counterbelief to the modern philanthropy that strives to increase life and relieve suffering. But Nietzsche also articulated something equally disquieting: an acid account of the sources of this modern philanthropy, of the mainsprings of this compassion and sympathy that powers the impressive enterprises of modern solidarity.

Nietzsche's "genealogy" of modern universalism, of the concern for the relief of suffering, of "pity," will probably not convince any people who have the highest examples of Christian agape or Buddhist *karuna* before their eyes. But the question remains very much open as to whether this unflattering portrait doesn't capture the possible fate of a culture that has aimed higher than its moral sources can sustain.

This is the issue I raised very briefly in the last chapter of *Sources*. The more impressed one is with this colossal extension of a gospel ethic to a universal solidarity, to a concern for human beings on the other side of the globe whom we shall never meet or need as companions or compatriots—or, because that is not the ultimate difficult challenge, the more impressed we are at the sense of justice we can still feel for people we do have contact with and tend to dislike or despise, or at a willingness to help people who often seem to be the cause of their own suffering—the more we contemplate all this, the more surprise we can feel at people who generate the motivation to engage in these enterprises of solidarity, international philanthropy, or the modern welfare state or, to bring out the negative side, the less surprised we are when the motivation to keep these people going flags, as we see in the present hardening of feeling against the impoverished and disfavored in Western democracies.

We could put the matter this way: our age makes higher demands for solidarity and benevolence on people today than ever before. Never before have people been asked to stretch out so far, so consistently, so systematically, so as a matter of course, to the stranger outside the gates. A similar point can be made, if we look at the other dimension of the affirmation of ordinary life, that concerned with universal justice. Here, too, we are asked to maintain standards of equality that cover wider and wider classes of people, bridge more and more kinds of difference, impinge more and more in our lives. How do we manage to do it?

Perhaps we don't manage all that well, and the interesting and important question might run: how could we manage to do it? But at least to get close to the answer to this, we should ask: how do we do as well as we do, which, after all, at first sight seems in these domains of solidarity and justice much better than in previous ages?

1. Performance to these standards has become part of what we understand as a decent, civilized human life. We live up to them to the extent that we do because we would be somewhat ashamed of ourselves if we didn't. They have become part of our self-image, our sense of our own worth. Alongside this, we feel a sense of satisfaction and superiority when we contemplate others—our ancestors or contemporary illiberal societies—who didn't or don't recognize them.

But we sense immediately how fragile this is as a motivation. It makes our philanthropy vulnerable to the shifting fashion of media attention and the various modes of feel-good hype. We throw ourselves into the cause of the month, raise funds for this famine, petition the government to intervene in that grisly civil war, and then forget all about it next month, when it drops off the CNN screen. A solidarity ultimately driven by the giver's own sense of moral superiority is a whimsical and fickle thing. We are far, in fact, from the universality and unconditionality which our moral outlook prescribes.

We might envisage getting beyond this by a more exigent sense of our own moral worth, one that would require more consistency, a certain independence from fashion, and careful, informed attention to the real needs. This is part of what people working in nongovernmental organizations (NGOs) in the field must feel, who correspondingly look down on us TV-image-driven givers, as we do on the lesser breeds who don't respond to this type of campaign at all.

2. But the most exigent, lofty sense of self-worth has limitations. I feel worthy in helping people, in giving without stint. But what is worthy about helping people? It's obvious; as humans, they have a certain dignity. My feelings of self-worth connect intellectually and emotionally with my sense of the worth of human beings. Here is where modern secular humanism is tempted to congratulate itself. In replacing the low and demeaning picture of human beings as depraved, inveterate sinners and in articulating the potential of human beings for goodness and greatness, humanism not only has given us the courage to act for reform but also explains why this philanthropic action is so immensely worthwhile. The higher the human potential, the greater the enterprise of realizing it and the more the carriers of this potential are worthy of our help in achieving it.

However, philanthropy and solidarity driven by a lofty humanism, just as that which was driven often by high religious ideals, has a Janus face. On one side, in the abstract, one is inspired to act. On the other, faced with the immense disappointments of actual human performance and with the myriad ways in which real, concrete human beings fall short of, ignore, parody, and betray this magnificent potential, one experiences a growing sense of anger and futility. Are these people really worthy objects of all these efforts? Perhaps in the face of all this stupid recalcitrance, it would not be a betrayal of human worth, or one's self-worth, to abandon them—or perhaps the best that can be done for them is to force them to shape up.

Before the reality of human shortcomings, philanthropy—the love of the human—can gradually come to be invested with contempt, hatred, aggression. The action is broken off or, worse, continues but is invested now with these new feelings, becoming progressively more coercive and inhumane. The history of despotic socialism (i.e., twentieth-century communism) is replete with this tragic turn, brilliantly foreseen by Dostoyevsky more than a hundred years ago ("Starting from unlimited freedom, I arrived at unlimited despotism"[7]), and then repeated again and again with a fatal regularity, through one-party régimes on a macro level, to a host of "helping" institutions on a micro level from orphanages to boarding schools for aboriginals.

The ultimate stop on the line was reached by Elena Ceauşescu in her last recorded statement before her murder by the successor régime: that the Romanian people have shown themselves unworthy of the immense, untiring efforts of her husband on their behalf.

The tragic irony is that the higher the sense of potential, the more grievously do real people fall short and the more severe the turnaround that is inspired by the disappointment. A lofty humanism posits high standards of self-worth and a magnificent goal to strive toward. It inspires enterprises of great moment. But by this very token it encourages force, despotism, tutelage, ultimately contempt, and a certain ruthlessness in shaping refractory human material—oddly enough, the same horrors that Enlightenment critique picked up in societies and institutions dominated by religion, and for the same causes.

The difference of belief here is not crucial. Wherever action for high ideals is not tempered, controlled, and ultimately engulfed in an unconditional love of the beneficiaries, this ugly dialectic risks repetition. And, of course, just holding the appropriate religious beliefs is no guarantee that this will be so.

3. A third pattern of motivation, which we have seen repeatedly, this time occurs in the register of justice rather than benevolence. We have seen it with Jacobins and Bolsheviks and today with the politically correct left and the so-called Christian right. We fight against injustices that cry out to heaven for vengeance. We are moved by a flaming indignation against these: racism, oppression, sexism, or leftist attacks on the family or Christian faith. This indignation comes to be fueled by hatred for those who support and connive with these injustices, which, in turn, is fed by our sense of superiority that we are not like these instruments and accomplices of evil. Soon, we are blinded to the havoc we wreak around us. Our picture of the world has safely located all evil outside us. The very energy and hatred with which we combat evil prove its exteriority to us. We must never relent but, on the contrary, double our energy, vie with each other in indignation and denunciation.

Another tragic irony nests here. The stronger the sense of (often correctly identified) injustice, the more powerfully this pattern can become entrenched. We become centers of hatred, generators of new modes of injustice on a greater scale, but we started with the most exquisite sense of wrong, the greatest passion for justice and equality and peace.

A Buddhist friend of mine from Thailand briefly visited the German Greens. He confessed to utter bewilderment. He thought he understood the goals of the party: peace between human beings and a stance of respect and friendship by humans toward nature. What astonished him was all the anger, the tone of denunciation and hatred toward the established parties. These people didn't seem to see that the first step toward their goal would have to involve stilling the anger and aggression in themselves. He couldn't understand what they were up to.

The blindness is typical of modern exclusive secular humanism. This modern humanism prides itself on having released energy for philanthropy and reform; by getting rid of "original sin," of a lowly and demeaning picture of human nature, it encourages us to reach high. Of course, there is some truth in this, but it is also terribly partial and terribly naive because it has never faced the questions I have been raising here: what can power this great effort at philanthropic reform? This humanism leaves us with our own high sense of self-worth to keep us from backsliding, a high notion of human worth to inspire us forward, and a flaming indignation against wrong and oppression to energize us. It cannot appreciate how problematic all of these are, how easily they can slide into something trivial, ugly, or downright dangerous and destructive.

A Nietzschean genealogist can have a field day here. Nothing gave Nietzsche greater satisfaction than showing how morality or spirituality is really powered by its direct opposite—for example, that the Christian aspiration to love is really motivated by the hatred of the weak for the strong. Whatever one thinks of this judgment on Christianity, it is clear that modern humanism is full of potential for such disconcerting reversals: from dedication to others to self-indulgent, feel-good responses, from a lofty sense of human dignity to control powered by contempt and hatred, from absolute freedom to absolute despotism, from a flaming desire to help the oppressed to an incandescent hatred for all those who stand in the way. And the higher the flight, the farther the potential fall.

Perhaps, after all, it's safer to have small goals rather than great expectations and to be somewhat cynical about human potentiality from the start. This is undoubtedly so, but then one also risks not having the motivation to undertake great acts of solidarity and to combat great injustices. In the end, the question becomes a maximum one: how to have the greatest degree of philanthropic action with the minimum hope in mankind. A figure like Dr. Rieu in Camus' *La Peste* stands as a possible solution to this problem. But that is fiction. What is possible in real life?

I said earlier that just having appropriate beliefs is no solution to these dilemmas, and the transformation of high ideals into brutal practice was demonstrated lavishly in Christendom, well before modern humanism came on the scene. So is there a way out?

This cannot be a matter of guarantee, only of faith. But it is clear that Christian spirituality points to one. It can be described in two ways: either as a love or compassion that is unconditional—that is, not based on what you the recipient have made of yourself—or as one based on what you are most profoundly, a being in the image of God. They obviously amount to the same thing. In either case, the love is not conditional on the worth realized in you just as an individual or even in what is realizable in you alone. That's because being made in the image of God, as a feature of each human being, is not something that can be characterized just by reference to this being alone. Our being in the image of God is also our standing among others in the stream of love, which is that facet of God's life we try to grasp, very inadequately, in speaking of the Trinity.

Now, it makes a whole lot of difference whether you think this kind of love is a possibility for us humans. I think it is, but only to the extent that we open ourselves to God, which means, in fact, overstepping the limits set in theory by exclusive humanisms. If one does believe that, then one has something very important to say to modern times, something that addresses the fragility of what all of us, believers and unbelievers alike, most value in these times.

Can we try to take stock of the first leg of our strange Ricci-like journey into the present? The trip is obviously not complete. We have just looked at some facets of modernity: the espousal of universal and unconditional rights, the affirmation of life, universal justice and benevolence. Important as these are, there are plainly others—for instance, freedom and the ethic of authenticity,[8] to mention just two. Nor have I had time to examine other dark features of modernity, such as its drive toward instrumental reason and control. But I think an examination of these other facets would show a similar pattern. So I'd like to try to define this more closely.

In a sense, our journey was a flop. Imitating Ricci would involve taking ourselves a distance from our time, feeling as strange in it as he felt as he was arriving in China. But what we saw as children of Christendom was, first, something terribly familiar—certain intimations of the gospel, carried to unprecedented lengths—and second, a flat negation of our faith, exclusive humanism. But still, like Ricci, we were bewildered. We had to struggle to make a discernment, as he did. He wanted to distinguish between those things in the new culture that came from the natural knowledge we all have of God and thus should be affirmed and extended, on one hand, and those practices that were distortions and would have to be changed, on the other. Similarly, we are challenged to a difficult discernment, trying to see what in modern culture reflects its furthering of the gospel, and what its refusal of the transcendent.

The point of my Ricci image is that this is not easy. The best way to try to achieve it is to take at least some relative distance, in history if not in geography. The danger is that we will not be sufficiently bewildered, that we think we have it all figured out from the start and know what to affirm and what to deny. We then can enter smoothly into the mainstream of a debate that is already going on in our society about the nature and value of modernity. As I have indicated,[9] this debate tends to become polarized between "boosters" and "knockers," who either condemn or affirm modernity en bloc, thus missing what is really at stake here, which is how to rescue admirable ideals from sliding into demeaning modes of realization.

From the Christian point of view, the corresponding error is to fall into one of two untenable positions: either we pick certain fruits of modernity, like human rights, and take them on board but then condemn the whole movement of thought and practice that underlies them, in particular the breakout from Christendom (in earlier variants, even the fruits were condemned), or, in reaction to this first position, we feel we have to go all the way with the boosters of modernity and become fellow travelers of exclusive humanism.

Better, I would argue, after initial (and, let's face it, still continuing) bewilderment, we would gradually find our voice from within the achievements of modernity, measure the humbling degree to which some of the most impressive extensions of a gospel ethic depended on a breakaway from Christendom, and from within these gains try to make clearer to ourselves and others the tremendous dangers that arise in them. It is perhaps not an accident that the history of the twentieth century can be read either in a perspective of progress or in one of mounting horror. Perhaps it is not contingent that it is the century both of Auschwitz and Hiroshima and of Amnesty International and Médecins sans Frontières. As with Ricci, the gospel message to this time and society has to respond both to what in it already reflects the life of God and to the doors that have been closed against this life. And in the end, it is no easier for us than it was for Ricci to discern both correctly, even if for opposite reasons. Between us twentieth-century Catholics, we have our own variants of the Chinese rites controversy. Let us pray that we do better this time.

Notes

1. This is not to say that we cannot claim in certain areas to have gained certain insights and settled certain questions that still troubled our ancestors. For instance, we are able to see the Inquisition clearly for the unevangelical horror that it was. But this doesn't exclude our having a lot to learn from earlier ages as well, even from people who also made the mistake of supporting the Inquisition.

2. Henri Bremond, *Histoire littéraire du sentient religieux en France depuis la fin des guerres de religion jusqu'à nos jours* (Paris: A. Colin, 1967–1968).

3. See *Sources of the Self* (Cambridge: Harvard University Press, 1989), chap. 13.

4. Cf. Daniel Callahan, *Setting Limits: Medical Goals in an Aging Society* (Washington, D.C.: Georgetown University Press, 1995).

5. James Miller, *The Passion of Michel Foucault* (New York: Simon & Schuster, 1993).

6. See René Girard, *La Violence et le Sacré* (Paris: Grasset, 1972); and *Le Bouc Emissaire* (Paris: Grasset, 1982).

7. Fyodor Dostoyevsky, *The Devils,* trans. David Magarshack (Harmondsworth, Middlesex: Penguin, 1971), 404.

8. Which I have discussed in *The Malaise of Modernity* (Toronto: Anansi, 1991); American edition: *The Ethics of Authenticity* (Cambridge: Harvard University Press, 1992).

9. Ibid.

2

"A Vote of Thanks to Voltaire"

• • •

WILLIAM M. SHEA

Having left the warm embrace of the Catholic University of America and arrived in the religiously chillier, and more bracing, atmosphere of a branch of the Florida state university system in 1980, I took an office across from a professor of classical cultures and Judaica. Al Gessmann, who may well have been a Catholic as a child, became a Jew after Hitler had begun his persecution and somehow managed to avoid being killed, though he lived those terrible years in Central Europe. Professor Gessmann was also a son of the rationalist Enlightenment, a devotee of the *Religionsgeschichte Schule*, a delighted observer of the American religious scene, and a man of vigorous opinions, such as the claim that Moses was an early rationalist and Judaism (at least as practiced by Al himself!) falls within the limits of reason alone. What struck me most, however, was his view that Catholicism is the most mythological version of Christianity and his surprise that, with my secular education and "rational interests" (many who know me would not agree with him on the latter), I could be a "practicing" Catholic.

A few years later, I ran into a similar perception of the relationship between an enlightened mind and Catholic faith and practice when I walked across campus with a woman participating in a conference on ethics education. She was editor of a journal of formerly Episcopalian and then socialist attachment and, when she determined that I was a Catholic and a professor in a state university, said: "I shall never understand how any educated person can be a Catholic."

These two people helped sharpen my already well-developed sense of the strains still evident in the late-twentieth-century United States between the Catholic religion and the culture born of the Enlightenment.[1] If I had thought in all innocence that I was modern, it became clear to me early on that others do not think so, that Catholic belief and practice constitute a problem for people outside the tribe. They look on me, I suspect, the way many of my kind look on Mormons and Jehovah's Witnesses. Much of my academic and personal energy over the past thirty years—since entering Columbia University's doctoral program in the study of religion—has been devoted to understanding and living with that strain between my religion and my culture. Michael J. Lacey of the Wilson Center put his finger on this "double consciousness" of Catholics.

> In broad cultural terms, Catholics, too, have long been regarded by America's non-Catholic intellectual elites as something of a problem. It is only the difficulty of "rightly framing the question," to use DuBois's phrasing, that has spared us from being asked more often what it feels like to be a member of a backward race, intellectually speaking, with an old world mumbo-jumbo all our own, fraught with formalism and clericalism, and marked by a communal history that was shaped in America by a spirit of defensiveness and the feeling, so long evident to outsiders, of being beleaguered by the main currents in modern thought. Like African Americans, Catholics, too, have long been uncomfortably conscious of being watched, of a kind of cultural surveillance in which the condition of their minds and hearts was monitored not only by Rome, but by many impressive and perhaps equally well intentioned non-Catholic communities as well. As a result, Catholics, too, have experienced the sense, as DuBois put it, ". . . of always looking at oneself through the eyes of others, of measuring one's soul by the tape of a world that looks on in amused contempt and pity."[2]

Modernity, modernism, modernization, and postmodernism present a terminological thicket that brings joy to the heart of a philosopher. I shall stipulate what I take to be Taylor's usage of a couple of these terms. To specify briefly my own views at the outset, let me say that classic Catholic modernism at the beginning of the century was correct in its intention, occasionally brilliant in its execution, and made its tragic mistake in subordinating the doctrinal tradition, the teaching authority of bishops, and theology to the court ruled by historical investigation, and that postmodernism is an unfortunate term for an interesting and even predictable reappearance of Enlightenment skepticism. I do not think that postmodernism is a decisive break with or advance over modernity or the other phases of the Enlightenment. In some ways, it is a retreat from the achievements of the moderate, naturalist, and pragmatist phase of the Enlightenment prevailing in the United States in the first half of the twentieth century. Postmodern theory's decline over the past few years has been matched by a vigorous reassertion of the intention of American philosophers to speak to significant ethical, political, and social problems. In this, the current inheritors of the classical American modernist philosophies join Catholic thinkers such as Alasdair MacIntyre and Taylor himself.[3]

Reflective religious modernization is essential for Catholics if the achievements of Vatican II are to be supported and extended. The term for the task of reflective modernization is *systematic theology*, a moment in theology (distinct from the historical and the practical moments) in which the theologian attempts to make intellectual sense of Christian tradition in his or her cultural context.[4] Discussions of the Church and modernity, then, fall under systematics.[5]

Two judgments are crucial to systematic efforts at revision of the Church's stance toward modernity. First, modernity has not been all wrong and, second, the Church has not been all right in the struggles of the past two centuries. One might well push the judgment a bit further: modernity has been quite right and the Church quite wrong about some very important matters (and vice versa), for example, the importance of critical history and of the self-determination of peoples. One must leave the apportioning of praise and blame to valuative history[6] in its retelling of the tale of modernity and the Roman Catholic Church, but we have quietly now put aside the more florid rhetoric of each side—namely, the Catholic claim that modernity expresses its true meaning in twentieth-century totalitarianism and the Enlightenment claim that the papacy and the church are irreformably obscurantist and antidemocratic. Once one has achieved these key insights, essays at untangling the relationship become plausible. With full recognition of the sins and graces of each, finger-pointing can be suspended, and dialogue and exploration can continue. Short of these judgments, each side will continue its investigative reporting on the faults of the other.

Let me begin with a review of some of Charles Taylor's points to be sure that I am not straying from his message. Then I shall add some comments to his story and point to the Catholic university as the test case of the relationship between Catholicism and modernity, a relationship that carries tensions old and new.

Retelling Taylor's Story

Modernity, Taylor tells us, must be seen to include the espousal of universal and unconditional human rights and the affirmation of life, universal justice, benevolence, freedom, and the ethic of authenticity. It also has its dark features, such as a drive toward instrumental reason and control. Taylor distinguishes as well between the *fact* of modernity and two *theories* of modernity.[7] The fact of modernity is the cultural shift that has been taking place over the past few centuries, whereas the theories of modernity offer explanations of and, in one case, myths about that shift. Taylor has a theory about modernity that markedly differs from the Enlightenment package that is standard among philosophers and Western cultural elites. It is important to realize this, for otherwise his remarks on a proper Catholic attitude toward modernity will be misunderstood.

He disagrees vigorously with what he calls an "accultural theory," proposes his own "cultural theory," and consequently looks upon modernity with an equanimity and detachment that would make my Catholic teachers uncomfortable. Modernity for him does not mean the revolutionary occurrence of a set of value-neutral facts and the consequent replacement of one set of beliefs (traditional and mythic) with another (modern and scientific), as the accultural explanation would have it. Modernity rather originated in a shift in

"A VOTE OF THANKS TO VOLTAIRE"

our horizons of understanding of humanity, the cosmos, society, and God and constituted an unarticulated background against which changes, as well as continuities, of practice and beliefs stand out and must be understood.[8]

It is not important at this moment to get the sweep and depth of what Taylor is proposing in this regard, although it is both broad and deep and deserves the attention of any person interested in the puzzle of the remarkable and ironic success of religions in contemporary cultures, the Catholic Church not least among them. I mean to note here only that he has worked out an illuminating philosophical understanding of the phenomenon of modernity and that it is in the light of this theory that he argues that Catholics can participate constructively in it. In other words, modernity for Taylor does not mean what "the modern world" seems to have meant to Pius X and the popes before and immediately after him[9] any more than it means what the acculturists take it to mean. Although their evaluations differ, many nineteenth- and twentieth-century Catholic leaders and Enlightenment acculturists mean the very same thing, and they are both mistaken. At the very least, it must be said that modernity obviously does not imply the end of Catholicism (and other premodern religions).

But neither is Taylor proposing a "Catholic modernism"—that is, that Catholics accept the accultural understanding of the emergence of the modern world and the dogmas of the Enlightenment ("the Enlightenment package"). Nor is he proposing a "modern Catholicism," one that supersedes its more or less benighted predecessors, as some liberal Catholics at times seem to suggest. Rather, he urges a "Catholic modernity"—that is, a full and critical participation in Western culture(s), acting on a citizenship long denied Catholics by the "cultured despisers" of the Church and, in their own way, by Catholic leaders. The proposal squares nicely with what I take to be the intention of the Second Vatican Council, the last three popes, and, most surely, the U.S. bishops.[10] It also aptly describes Taylor's own practice of philosophy and the aims of many theologians. It constitutes the attitude and hope of what I call reflective religious modernism.

Taylor's altogether healthy and sensible prescription carries with it a puzzle, however, for one is driven to wonder how Catholics can participate fully in this culture without drowning in it intellectually and spiritually, that is, how they can be Catholic in a culture that seems antireligious and anti-Catholic, whose life forms and practices undercut the forms and practices of historical Catholicism, and whose power of attraction threatens to become a power of compulsion? No one should underrate the dangers posed to religious insight and freedom by the manifold perversities of this culture of ours.

To look at it from another perspective, supposing a successful engagement with modernity, can Catholics hold back from a campaign to restore Christendom, a hope they set aside only in the past thirty years? Here we have the alternatives presented in the past by Catholic integralists and by anti-Catholic secularists and Protestants. Neither group, it must be said, lacked evidence to support its judgment that Catholic participation in modern life is impossible. No matter how absurd these alternatives appear in the face of the actual experience and history of Catholics "in the streets," we have not come so far in the past three decades that we no longer can hear and be moved by these ghosts.[11] When my professor friend and the socialist editor spoke, they touched a sore point in my own psyche, sensitive as I always am to that "amused contempt and pity" mentioned by Michael Lacey.

Taylor's proposed solution is the burden of his lecture at the University of Dayton.[12] He enunciates a version of the Catholic principle: "Catholic" means universality through wholeness, a wholeness constituted by complementarity rather than identity of parts. Wholeness is a unity of parts rather than a suppression of them. Suppressing diversity in human cultures is not the way to unity, to true Catholicism. Catholic unity embraces difference rather than fusing difference into identity. Trinitarian life is a unity of this kind.

This is a neat, if abstract, proposal that fits well with inherited understandings of Catholicism as it meets contemporary facts and reflections on cultural, social, and religious pluralism.[13] It also enunciates the (not untroubled) practice of the Church's leadership over the past thirty-five years. The degree of abstraction lessens somewhat when he explains that to "widen the faith" involves "an increase in the variety of devotions, spiritualities, liturgical forms, and responses to the Incarnation." Taylor recognizes that the Catholic Church does not have any better than a spotty record in such matters, for even the story of Matteo Ricci (which he fixes as the emblem of his argument for inculturation) reveals the weighty tradition of Roman conservatism and centralism, as well as Ricci's daring. But he also recognizes that the field of spiritualities now before us can save us from narrowness and make us recognize our partiality.

In other words, Catholics have agreed to an acceptance of pluralism both within and outside the church, though as Bernard Lonergan said about us, "arriving on the scene a little breathlessly and a little late."[14] In fact, modernity itself is not entirely alien to Catholics because it shows a Christian inheritance in its conviction of universal rights and its practice of universal philanthropy. On the one hand, we are strangers here, and on the other we are at home, facing a modernity which is at once disturbing and profoundly attractive to Catholic sensibilities. Shall we come to this saying "Whoever is not with me is against me" (Matt 12:30) or "Whoever is not against us is for us" (Mark 9:40)?

Taylor makes a historical judgment at this point. "Breaking with Christendom" (i.e., with the medieval Catholic and early modern Protestant practice of mutual support of state and church) was necessary if certain elements of Christian faith were themselves to be liberated. These elements flower in modern ideals of universal human rights to life, freedom, citizenship, and self-realization. Christendom was a marriage of faith, society, and culture ultimately doomed to frustration; it brought Christianity closer to forms of religion in which the sacred was bound up with and supported the secular.[15] What I would call the religious tribalism of Christians (identification of religion and culture, accompanied by a classicist understanding of cultural and religious normativity) needed to be ended if human beings, no matter their culture and religion, were to be seen as equal bearers of rights.[16] But Christendom as an ideal has proved resilient. Witness its importance in preconciliar twentieth-century Catholicism and current conservative American Protestant hankering after a "Christian America."

In Taylor's view, all ideologies, including Christianity, fail when identified with a culture, for ideologies will use the coercive force of the state to support their insistence on wholeness through identity (Jacobinism, Marxism, and Fascism are no improvement over Christendom in this respect).[17] The public sphere must be run by no one ideology; rather, it must be the sphere for competing ultimate visions, and so Taylor's "vote of thanks to Voltaire" for prompting Christians "to live the gospel in a purer way free of a 'bloody forcing of conscience'" brought on by the demand for identity.[18]

The end of Christendom, however, was accompanied by the rise of exclusive humanism (one of the ideologies offering an explanation and a myth for the cultural change taking place), which recognizes no valid aim beyond human flourishing and requires a "spiritual lobotomy" to cut off transcendence.[19]

According to Taylor, on the Catholic side of the modern equation, the task is to discern what "in the new culture came from the natural knowledge we all have of God . . . and those practices which were distortions" between "what in modern culture reflects . . . the gospel and what [reflects] its refusal of the gospel." Catholics need be neither "boosters" nor "knockers" of modern culture; rather, we are participants who are attempting to rescue admirable ideals from sliding into demeaning modes of practice.[20]

In Taylor's view, exclusive humanists have a bit of discerning to do as well. No matter how one puts the notion of transcendence, whether "something beyond life" or even "a radical change in oneself" in the light of transcendence, to deny it is to threaten the very flourishing that humanism means to protect and extend. Just as churches that bless "ordinary life and human flourishing" to the detriment of transcendence find themselves facing religious reformers calling for renewed renunciation in the name of transcendence and purity,[21] so also exclusive humanism, concerned with ordinary existence and its flourishing, will find itself contradicted from within by "neo-Nietzscheans" (Bataille, Foucault, Derrida) who challenge the primacy of ordinary life and offer precious little support for human flourishing. In Taylor's view, a religious affirmation of transcendence alone is not enough, nor is affirmation of life alone enough. Love of what is beyond life and love of life are bound together (the greatest and the second commandments of the Law). Give up either one, and violence, even a cult of suffering and death, results within religion, as well as in secular society.

There are, then, four parties in the contemporary debate: (1) exclusive humanists, (2) neo-Nietzschean antihumanists, and (3 and 4) those who acknowledge a good beyond life, some of whom (3) are opposed to the move to the primacy of life in exclusive humanism (Catholic integralists and Protestant fundamentalists?) and (4) some of whom think the practical primacy of life has been a great gain, that there are legitimate values inherent in modern culture, and that there is some truth in the "revolutionary story"—namely, for a rights culture to exist, a break with the established religion was necessary. Taylor belongs to the fourth party. The directness with which he states and argues this position is gratifying.

A Gloss to Taylor's Story

Tribalism is, of course, a human and not just a Christian or religious condition: it involves, in various cultural and social settings, an identification of normative humanity with one's bloodline, one's group, one's practice, one's beliefs. Typically, it places one's group at the center of the universe and of human and even divine history. The *Enuma Elish*, for example, is primarily a tale of the ascendancy of Babylon that is concerned only in a weakened sense with the genealogy of the gods. Perhaps the papal documents on the ordination of women will likewise be judged political rather than religious documents, though much is made in them of divinely intended traditions. Admittedly, tribalism augurs well for one's survival in certain situations, but it hardly contributes to welcoming the stranger, nor does it celebrate difference. Tribalism, of course, survived the end of Christendom in the West, not least in the fact that the universalism proclaimed in the Enlightenment extended only in principle and legally to Catholic Christians and Jews and other such unenlightened folk, surely not in cultural fact. The enlightened themselves, despite their intentions, constituted another tribe, as have their postmodernist great-grandchildren. It is difficult, once one has seen the light, to treat the blind as sighted.

The Catholic Church has been at war, hot and cold, with the enlightened and the Protestant tribes. The existence of those tribes, undoing Christendom in all but dream and insisting that they were, in fact, at the center of human and divine history, was taken to be of apocalyptic significance by Catholic leaders. Though primarily an interest of the Church's leadership rather than of the Catholic masses, the struggle nonetheless molded Catholic thought and practice for four hundred years. The war and the molding ended at the Second Vatican Council, though it must be said that the council was long in the making and tumultuous in its outcomes. Like other councils, Vatican II solved a problem, closed an era, laid out a direction, and so began a new era for the Church.

What exactly did happen between 1962 and 1965? Did the war end?[22] In a cease-fire? A truce? A surrender from exhaustion? A pragmatic alliance for common ends and/or a feint on the part of Church leaders to meet a requirement for participation in contemporary politics? Or is there something to this of an intellectual nature, with a truth involved? Did Catholics learn something? Did and does the end require a conversion of mind and heart on all sides? Yes, many Catholics did learn something: counterculture is not the Catholic norm, and modernity, though its light is far from pure, is not a moral black hole. Yes, the end to the centuries-long struggle requires a conversion of imagination and mind. Yes, it has proven possible to end a war and join the former enemy in a common struggle for justice and truth.

The successes of the council are so enormous that one might well ask why we are still talking about modernity and the modern world as if they were something other than ourselves. The heirs of the Reformation and the Enlightenment have begun to recast their images of the Catholic Church. Even some American evangelicals, those offspring of Puritan suspicion of works righteousness, have recently shown signs of recognizing Catholics as Christians.[23] The Church, too, has begun to reconfigure its relationship to both and has radically revised its image of the modern world, although initiating this turn of the tide has not been entirely successful on the Catholic side, at least among the clerical leadership.

What are the basic terms of the settlement with modernity on the Catholic side? Let me list a few crucial propositions formulated on the basis of the Church's follow-through since the council.

1. The initiative and cooperation of the laity are suffered by the clergy to a degree nearly unimaginable prior to the council. For example, it is hard to imagine the hierarchy launching an anti–birth control campaign now; even its vigorous anti-abortion campaign is muted in comparison with what it once would have been and is conducted on the basis of a politics of persuasion.[24] In addition, laity now administer and govern many Church-sponsored institutions, such as hospitals, schools, colleges, and charities.

2. The sciences are viewed as entirely and permanently insulated from criticism by Church leaders. Clerical leaders have given up attempting to squeeze the sciences into a scriptural, doctrinal, or theological mold and are now given to apologies to dead geniuses and even to reformers. The point is not that this or that theory or scientist or extrascientific oracle by scientists will not be excoriated

or praised by this or that theologian or hierarch but that there is universal recognition that the sciences must take care of their own business. While subject to ethical critique, they are no longer to be criticized on doctrinal grounds.

3. The hierarchy has made the decisive move to approval of democratic politics. The distance in conception of the proper organization of society from that of Pius IX and even Leo XIII to that of John Paul II is enormous and irreversible. Human rights and the "rights of peoples to self-determination" have become Vatican causes. It strikes me that some of what John Paul II teaches as a matter of course would have Pius IX spinning in his grave. This signals the correctness of Taylor's view that the change is primarily cultural. What permits such historically uncharacteristic utterance is the fact that the change in cultural horizon has overwhelmed the church's leaders. After two hundred years of pillorying democratic politics, the bishops, perhaps moved in this case by "the American experiment," have changed their mind on the promise of democracy for humanity and Catholicism.

4. Church leaders have shown scrupulous regard for the political rights and reputations of even those who oppose their views. With few exceptions, opponents are treated as fellow citizens and their consciences respected, rather than as traitors, reprobates, or barbarian occupiers of a culture not their own. Antimodernist rhetoric has fallen by the wayside. Criticism of public policy and practice is now couched in language that draws on common and contemporary human ideals, rather than the language of Christendom.

5. *Cultures* is a key term in the documents of the current pope, a man whose own Polish culture was under threat of extinction from successive alien ideologies. The recognition of the value and the rights of cultures to survival and some political autonomy is joined to a newly reformed understanding of "evangelization" that downplays incorporation of cultures into the Latin form of Christianity and plays up "inculturation of the gospel," a change of terminology that displays a grasp of contemporary sensibilities toward social realities—joined by occasional warnings against "overinculturation" and relativism.

Though some would interpret all these changes as a surrender to modernity, they are much more likely due to a recognition of the legitimate autonomy of cultures by the Church, forced by historical circumstance, no doubt, but nonetheless profound and genuine. The dream of Christendom, to use Taylor's term, has ended, and with it hierarchical conceptions of social order.

Catholic theologians' reaction to the changes over the past three decades is a mixed bag. There is a much more sophisticated methodological atmosphere among them, but they remain institutionally introverted. (I do not except myself and this essay!) The typical program of the Catholic Theological Society of America, for example, is relentlessly ecclesiocentric in its focus.

The exceptions are many, of course, but the outstanding ones in the English speaking Catholic theological world are Bernard Lonergan and David Tracy, whose influential careers span the past half century. Lonergan represented a careful and critical engagement with modernity and its chief intellectual shapers on the most basic theoretic levels, with barely a touch of the antimodernist and anti-Enlightenment rhetoric on which Catholics of his generation were all raised. He was immensely bothered by clerical anti-intellectualism and needed little other experience than membership in the Jesuits to spark his critique of the bias of common sense against theory.[25] Granted that he had tremendous fun in *Insight* with the blunders of Hume and Kant, Lonergan saw that there were genuine intellectual problems forced on Christian thinkers and set about solving them rather than attacking the enemy.

David Tracy represents the public achievement and the goal of Catholic postconciliar intellectuals, including theologians: full participation as equals in contemporary intellectual culture conducted on the basis of both religious conviction and knowledge of Western intellectual figures and movements. None of Lonergan's students better embody his definition of theology as a mediation between church and culture.[26] Tracy and theologians like him intend to act as a Christian voice in contemporary culture, partaking in the conversation rather than taking it over. Charles Taylor himself is an outstanding example of a Catholic's engagement in current philosophical problems in a contemporary idiom and with a powerful sense of the liberation provided by a religious tradition.

The present pope, despite his much vaunted reversion to pre–Vatican II authoritarianism, is in this line: a vigorous intellectual and spiritual participant in the culture formation of the modern world. Pius IX and his predecessors saw modernity (modern forms of belief and practice) as the enemy and consequently mis-led the church in this war. Pope John Paul II, whom some Catholics see primarily as a restorationist, is, in fact, an excellent example of Catholic critical engagement with modern culture, a truly modern man with firm roots in a tradition and a community, who joins the public exchange, who backs down from no one, and who shows respect to all,[27] refusing to trace present problems and aberrations to the perversions of the Protestant "revolt" and the Enlightenment, as did his preconciliar predecessors.

On the other "side," John Dewey is the prime example of Taylor's exclusive humanism and its affirmation of ordinary life. He broke gradually and smoothly with the Christian church in his adult years because his maturing philosophical views no longer found adequate expression in Christian terms or even, as time went by, correlation with them.[28] His late book, *A Common Faith*, makes it clear that at that time (1934) the stumbling block for him was doctrines that the churches took for statement of fact and thereby set themselves as the judges of science.

Taylor remarks that the problem of transcendence in the modern world is moral and spiritual rather than epistemic. In Dewey's case, the problem is both. Christianity seemed to him incapable of supporting a world-transforming practice of the method of intelligence. But this weakness is also a significant epistemic problem—namely, that religious belief, if construed as cognitive, has no relation to available data. Dewey remained, on this issue at least, an empiricist. Even though he and other exclusive humanists developed elaborate theoretic rationales to explain the human devotion to the transcendent and to justify it, in the end Dewey's philosophical resolution strikes me as naive, unworthy, and even shallow. Dewey lost as much intellectually by his abandonment of the church as the church lost when he abandoned it.

For this discussion, the interesting thing about Dewey is that, as clearly as he was an heir of the Enlightenment and of liberalism (his early work centered around Leibniz, Kant, Hegel, and J. S. Mill), Dewey was a communitarian who learned his communitarianism and localism in American congregational Christianity and who, on its basis, was forthrightly and powerfully critical of standard liberalism and individualism.[29] Although neither he nor other naturalists were at all well disposed toward traditional religions and surely do espouse at certain points the accultural understanding of modernity and look on the church as a relic, they also display signs, marked by Taylor, of a residual Christian spirituality and sensibility.[30] The leading American social theorist Philip Selznick promotes a communitarian tradition and remains a convinced naturalist.[31] All of this calls into question the simplistic Catholic anti-modernist and anti-Enlightenment rhetoric that demonized Dewey and continued the excoriations of the Enlightenment up to the eve of the council.

But the heirs of the Reformation and the Enlightenment are as complex intellectually and spiritually as are the heirs of the Catholic anti-modernists. No more can the Enlightenment and its exclusive humanism be captured in a single descriptor than can the Catholicism that confronted it. Claiming that Catholicism as a whole was integralist even in the days of the antimodernist crusade is a historical distortion. The humanists (American naturalist philosophy is humanism's articulation) have made serious intellectual efforts to come to grips with religious traditions and their social and cultural impact.[32] If we are thrown into some confusion about what happened at Vatican II and why, should we not lean to some modesty on just what happened in the origins of modernity and how it has progressed? Ought we not be driven to agree with Taylor that modernity is a mixed bag, and add that so, too, is historical and contemporary Catholicism? It is ironic that Catholics, who, their intellectuals tell us, are born and bred analogists, should so often fall under the spell of the dialectical imagination, which finds contradictions and tends to leave them as found, declaring one right and the other wrong. While the Enlightenment and Christian faith may at some points and in some historical manifestations be opposed, one can hope in advance that they will not be found opposed in every important matter.[33] Taylor finds that they are not.[34]

There are, it must be admitted, continuing deep enmities between some secularist and Protestant thinkers and some in the Catholic Church. On the eve of the council, the liberal Protestant case in the United States was made by Paul Blanshard: Catholicism as an enemy of democracy. On the conservative evangelical side, Loraine Boettner, as the council opened, saw the Church as an enemy of the Christian gospel.[35] As they were not the first, so they are not the last. Deweyan naturalist Sidney Hook continued to find religious belief itself alien to modern culture.[36] The outstanding twentieth-century Protestant thinkers, Reinhold Niebuhr, Paul

Tillich, and Karl Barth all retained suspicions of the incompatibility of Catholicism and Christianity, with good reason, for the Catholic documents and practices are there to provide a foundation for worry and doubt, every bit as much as the documents and deeds of the Enlightenment leaders gave Catholics good reason for concern and even enmity. No one "made up" this war; it really happened, even though it might not have with a pinch more wisdom on each side.

Mark Noll has written of "The Rise and Long Life of the Protestant Enlightenment in America" and the embrace of the moderate Enlightenment by the Protestant cultural and ministerial elites in the eighteenth and nineteenth centuries, a relationship that produced a hybrid of mainline Protestantism (modernism) at the turn of the twentieth century. The marriage also resulted in a vicious family squabble in the fundamentalist crisis of the first half of the twentieth century that paralleled the modernist crisis in the Catholic Church. In Noll's view, there was not sufficient critical assessment of the Enlightenment by Protestants, but rather an identification with it, its ideals, and its assumptions. To this day, according to Noll, evangelical Protestantism has failed to produce a major theoretical critique of the Enlightenment and an intellectual wrestling with the epistemological foundations of its now various phases.[37]

According to Patrick Carey, American Catholics passed through several phases in their attitudes toward the American (Protestant) Enlightenment and its cultural and social exclusion of Catholics. One can recognize a deep-seated animosity of many American Catholic leaders toward modernity. So strong was it that American Catholics developed their own "understanding of reason, the individual, community, church, state, freedom, authority, justice, the common good, and society."[38] In neither case, Protestant nor Catholic, is the relation to modernity simple or univocal. But both religious communities paid a very high price for their respective positions. Liberal Protestantism handed over "truth" to science, dropped the normative status of Christian revelation, and gave birth to Protestant modernism[39]; conservative Protestants fell into anti-intellectual fundamentalism; Catholics agreed to quasisect status in modern American culture and to a clergy rigidly educated and nearly without an intellectual life and then created their own subculture in its institutions, ranging from a separate school system to separate scholarly societies.[40]

But Taylor is in a position to propose a quite different strategy, one that flows from Vatican II and the last three popes (and is not in continuity with the preceding papal policies). Though laid out doctrinally in *Lumen Gentium* and *Gaudium et Spes*, the most impressive signs of the Catholic change are the documents on Jews and other religions (*Nostra Aetate*) and on the rights of conscience and worship (*Dignitatis Humanae*).[41] According to William Green, "The Enlightenment cut its teeth on the Jewish question,"[42] and so, too, did the conciliar Church. If Catholic "supersessionism" (the Christian doctrine that the church supersedes Israel in the history of salvation) could be abandoned and anti-Semitism condemned on theological and doctrinal grounds, if the Pope can pray with Hindus, if Catholic theologians will risk all to rethink the relations between the Church and Judaism, Islam, and other world religions, what closed door cannot be opened? This change is the prime condition for Catholic participation in modernity, and it is also the great sign of the doctrinal rethinking of Catholicism and modern culture.

This rethinking of human dignity, religion, and freedom reflects Taylor's mediating path: neither surrender nor rejection, neither "booster" nor "knocker," but participant, voice, critical engager, respecter of the rights of each person and each religious tradition, and one who admits (sometimes cautiously) that there is truth to be found in them. Most conservative Catholics, accused of ecclesiastical restorationism, and most liberal Catholics, charged with cultural assimilationism, are within the spectrum of the postconciliar affirmation of the world of modernity. Both fall under Taylor's Catholic principle that unite transcendence and justice.

The Catholic University and Modernity

The mediation of culture and Catholicism Taylor advocates is peculiarly the position and task of the Catholic universities and colleges. They serve as the prime instance of it and a test case for it. The roots of the contemporary American Catholic university and college are traceable to modernity as well as to Catholicism. They, too, have broken with Christendom and with the "bloody forcing of conscience," and for them, too, we owe "a vote of thanks to Voltaire."

But how can it be true to both roots, the Christian gospel and the Enlightenment's secularized intelligence, and be recognized as legitimate offspring by both? It *must* be both if it is to meet Taylor's catholic principle, yet it cannot be so without serious difficulty. Some would find Catholic higher education involved in a profound contradiction: academic freedom and a form of hierarchical direction are intrinsically opposed.[43] But the question of academic freedom and hierarchy is merely the lodestone for American academic worries over religiously affiliated institutions of higher education. To Catholic theologians and other humanities academics, who agree from the outset with Pope John Paul II that the Catholic university serves both humanity and the church and, in doing so, "is able to institute an incomparably fertile dialogue with people of every culture,"[44] the question might be phrased: To what extent and in what way is Catholicism in "the heart of the university" and the university in "the heart of the church"?[45] The answers may be many and will change over time, for church, university, and the cultures in which they are embedded are themselves living realities. In our American culture, with its vast system of institutions of higher education, certain problems are forced to the front, and they reflect the larger problem of the interaction of church and modern culture of which Taylor writes.

Among these culture-specific problems and questions are these: How does a university (which, after all, is *not* a church!) stand for the Christian gospel *and* for the hard-won intellectual and spiritual pluralism which it is the task of the contemporary university to defend and further as an achievement of modern Western culture, at the very time when the role and task of the American university itself is under fire? How can the Catholic university, in particular, avoid becoming a flea market of ideas and disciplines, on the one hand, or a traditionalist ecclesiastical redoubt, on the other? (There is no need for one and only one answer to this question.) How can it welcome all and thereby risk intellectual chaos and moral vacuity, on one hand, and on the other uphold a sacramental and communitarian Catholic viewpoint and thereby risk suspicions of ideological control on research and teaching?[46]

Can a Catholic university survive these tensions? Gregory Lucey, S.J., warned more than two decades ago that Marquette University had only a decade to decide its fate. Now others warn that the rest of the colleges and universities have only a decade to go.[47] William Miller was wrong about 1849, and our current academic apocalypticists are likely wrong about 2006. Although we do face some hard problems and decisions, I believe the Catholic university and college can and should (and will!) survive, precisely as the locus for the sometimes tense and often fruitful exchange between the church and modernity. It is a benefit for both our culture and the church that, however it is worked out, they should occupy the same space.

Catholic institutions can engage the culture in ways impossible for the large research universities (as their way is impossible for us) and display the harmony between religious commitment and democracy, between faith and reason, between low social status and the highest social and political ideals, between individual intellectual responsibility and communitarian practice and learning.[48] They can also question the Church's more than occasional introversion, its intellectual and spiritual mediocrity, its lack of interest in public discourse and process, and its inertial classicism by simply doing their job as a home for researchers and teachers and as a support and platform for Catholic intellectuals.

These ideals and this struggle over goals are embraced by *Ex Corde Ecclesiae* in principle (granted, practice is never as easy as principle), and the difficult and tangled relationship with the Church has been eased without complaint and with brotherly concern by the American bishops in their implementation of *Ex Corde*.[49] Both documents deserve the applause of everyone in the university as an affirmation of its mediating role along the lines marked off by Taylor.

Conclusion

There remains an unavoidable tension in Catholicism between renunciation and flourishing, transcendence and immanence, history and apocalyptic, Logos and mythos, and family and evangelization. The genius of Catholicism is that it chooses both horns. The tension is traceable to the early churches, of course, stretched out between the resurrection, which was to be the last act in this age, and the attempts at domestication of the churches by Constantine and Theodosius, during which the Catholic Church emerged.

But the root of the tension runs down into the figure and message of Jesus himself. He is the enigma. Jacob Neusner recently sketched an unforgettable portrait of the Jesus of Matthew's Gospel, bringing him into our history for a moment of dialogue over his Jewishness.[50] The infamous Jesus Seminar deals only with the surface ambiguities of the Jesus of historicism, whereas Neusner knows what the deep strain is: the figure of a Jesus who talks of grains dying and crosses to be carried, of cataclysms and turning our backs on our dead parents, of the plucking out of eyes and the cutting off of hands, while his Father of old has told us to increase, multiply, and fill the earth, plant a vine and an olive tree, and teach the children the rituals of memory and hope. No, the deep problem is not the so-called Jesus of history (as Neusner well knows) but the Jesus of the Church, crucified and risen from the dead, and straddling two aeons.

I do not suggest that we will or should get over this tension, but it must constantly be addressed by Catholic thinkers, most of whom find it desirable to raise the family, wise to keep a sharp eye on the prophet and the apocalypticist, and commonsensical to hesitate to follow leaders who may long for a doomed crusade against modern culture and for the return of Christendom. God knows the culture needs deep and abiding criticism, but God knows just as well that it is "our" culture and not "theirs." Living in the present, then, means evaluating and reconstructing the past, discerning what can be carried on and built upon, what must be reconfigured, and what has to be laid aside in the Church, as well as in the culture. Modernity, in this sense, is equivalent to historical consciousness with its concomitant historical responsibility. The past is not a toy, a prison, or a triumphal banner. In this sense, the Church must be modern, and from the cross of historical consciousness and its responsibilities it cannot come down. In this case, the Church and its universities have distinct and different roles to play in relation to culture.

The trouble will go on between the Church and its cultures—as it always has. The Church as a community will remain troubled, for its ambivalence about cultures will remain. The tensions can legitimately be addressed in rhetorical flourishes about the Incarnation, but they will be overcome at least in some moments by contemplation of the Crucified One. At bottom, the struggle is within the hearts and minds of Catholic women and men, who, under the strictures of modernity and the exigencies of faith, will be faithful to and critical of both Church and culture, letting go of neither and finding a way to live in and with both. This drama of the person is, in fact, the great drama—the quest of the Christian to keep body and soul together. Written large, it is the drama of the culture and the Church.

Notes

1. On the complexity of the Enlightenment tradition, see Henry May, *The Enlightenment in America* (New York: Oxford University Press, 1976). See also W. M. Shea, "Tradition and Pluralism: Opportunities for Catholic Universities," *Current Issues in Catholic Higher Education* 16/1 (Summer 1995): 334–48; and the essays in W. Shea and P. Huff, eds., *Knowledge and Belief in America: Enlightenment Traditions and Modern Religious Thought*. Woodrow Wilson Center Series (New York: Cambridge University Press, 1995).

2. Michael J. Lacey, "The Backwardness of American Catholicism," *Conversations on Jesuit Higher Education* 8 (Fall 1995): 6.

3. On the views of the contemporary Americans and their general fidelity to the older American naturalist-pragmatist tradition, see Giovanna Borradori, *The American Philosopher: Conversations with Quine, Putnam, Nozick, Danto, Rorty, Cavell, MacIntyre, and Kuhn* (Chicago: University of Chicago Press, 1994). The literature on pragmatism and Dewey has taken an exciting and constructive turn in the past decade. Among the most recent and on the subject at hand, see John Patrick Diggins, *The Promise of Pragmatism: Modernism and the Crisis of Knowledge and Authority* (Chicago: University of Chicago Press, 1994). Among contemporary Catholic philosophers, Alasdair MacIntyre is the best known critic of the Enlightenment; see *After Virtue: A Study in Moral Theory* (South Bend, Ind.: University of Notre Dame Press, 1981).

4. Bernard Lonergan distinguishes "systems" as a functional speciality in theology from others such as history and foundations, and its task is to make the Christian meanings available to the contemporary culture. See his *Method in Theology* (New York: Herder and Herder, 1972). Schubert Ogden distinguishes historical, systematic, and practical theology in "What Is Theology?" *Journal of Religion* 52 (1973): 22–40.

5. I shall capitalize *Church* in this chapter when it refers to the Roman Catholic Church, following the dictum of Lenny Bruce (may he rest in peace) to the effect that when anyone says, "the Church," everyone knows which church is being spoken of.

6. Longeran in *Method* (pp. 302, 312, 320) speaks of a history that evaluates developments on criteria drawn from intellectual, moral, and religious conversion.

7. "Two Theories of Modernity" in *Hastings Center Report* 25/2 (March–April 1995): 24–33. See also his books *The Ethics of Authenticity*

(Cambridge: Harvard University Press, 1992) and *Sources of the Self: The Making of the Modern Identity* (Cambridge: Harvard University Press, 1989).

8. See Lonergan's essay "The Problem of Belief Today" in *A Second Collection*, ed. by W. F. Ryan (Philadelphia: Westminster Press, 1974).

9. See Lester B. Kurtz, *The Politics of Heresy: The Modernist Crisis in Roman Catholicism* (Berkeley: University of California Press, 1986); Marvin R. O'Connell, *Critics on Trial: An Introduction to the Catholic Modernist Crisis* (Washington, D.C.: Catholic University of America Press, 1994); and R. Scott Appleby, *"Church and Age Unite!" The Modernist Impulse in American Catholicism* (South Bend, Ind.: University of Notre Dame Press, 1992).

10. The latter display that intention by their vigorous engagement in the "public" and "secular" issues of war and the economy, as well as with abortion, in all three cases on natural law (i.e., public) grounds. In two of the cases, modernity has had a significant impact on the bishops, and the same impact has been displayed in the recent solution of the bishops to the implementation of *Ex corde ecclesiae*. Careful and prolonged consultation of the interested and informed parties was crucial in these cases. I take this to be an example of their acceptance of what Taylor calls the rights culture. Of course, there are limits and even setbacks: Archbishop Rembert Weakland of Milwaukee and Cardinal Joseph Bernardin of Chicago were strongly criticized by some brother bishops for their suggestion of dialogue as a way to deal with painful divisions in the church over matters including sexual ethics. In the cases of sexual ethics, there is little evidence of consultation.

11. On the one hand, Pope John Paul warns us against the "culture of death," capitalism, and consumerism, the last two of which constitute the economic infrastructure of the culture. See *Evangelium Vitae* and *Centesimus Annus*. Cardinal Ratzinger uncovers postmodernist "relativism" as the chief enemy of Christian faith, while on the other hand some American evangelical Christians still see the Catholic Church as the enemy of "true" Christianity. See Joseph Cardinal Ratzinger, "Relativism: The Central Problem for Faith Today," in *Origins* 26 (October 31, 1996): 309–317. For contemporary evangelical statements, see James G. McCarthy, *The Gospel according to Rome: Comparing Catholic Tradition and the Word of God* (Eugene, Ore.: Harvest House, 1995); and John Ankerberg and John Weldon, eds., *Protestants and Catholics: Do They Now Agree?* (Eugene, Ore.: Harvest House, 1995).

12. The University of Dayton is an appropriate place for such a lecture, given its own important leadership in the transition of Catholic institutions of higher learning to a new conception of such things as academic freedom and the importance of the sciences to liberal education. See Philip Gleason, *Contending with Modernity: Catholic Higher Education in the Twentieth Century* (New York: Oxford University Press, 1995).

13. The principle is clearly related to the sacramental principle, the principle of subsidiarity, and current communion ecclesiology.

14. Lonergan. *Insight: A Study of Human Understanding* (New York: Philosophical Library, 1956), 733.

15. Darrell Fasching has systematically explored this distinction in his works in the Holocaust and Christian ethics. See his latest book, *The Coming of the Millennium: Good News for the Whole Human Race* (Valley Forge, Pa.: Trinity International Press, 1996), where he deals with the sacred and the holy in relation to cultures.

16. Perhaps the most painful and revealing battle within the Church since the council has been over whether, having accepted a "rights culture," the church must become to some degree a "rights church." On Catholic tribalism, see W. Shea, "Fundamentalism: How Catholics Approach It," in F. Nichols, *Christianity and the Stranger: Historical Essays* (Atlanta: Scholars Press, 1995) 221–286. See also *A Culture of Rights: The Bill of Rights in Philosophy, Politics, and Law. 1791–1991,* ed. M. Lacey and K. Haaksonssen (New York: Cambridge University Press, 1991).

17. We recall that the practice of ideology critique began with Protestant objections to the Papal claim to jurisdiction over Christian churches ("popery"). See Mark Goldie, "Ideology," in *Political Innovation and Conceptual Change,* ed. T. Ball, J. Farr, and R. Hanson (New York: Cambridge University Press, 1989), 266–291.

18. The Enlightenment, it must be said, retained a big belt of Christendom's classicism, as Taylor points out in "Two Theories of Modernity." Classicism runs through the accultural theory of modernity.

19. This is not entirely true, for many of the American philosophers of the golden age, naturalists and pragmatists among them, tried to explain what obviously could not be "cut off." Dewey, Santayana, Randall, Woodbridge, and James made constructive statements on the transcendent, as did many second-generation naturalists and pragmatists. A later pragmatism has regressed to the position that religion is not worth attention and its voice in theology need not be heard. See Richard Rorty, *Consequences of Pragmatism: Essays, 1972–1980,* (Minneapolis: University of Minnesota Press, 1982).

20. We must also have the concomitant task of discerning what in Catholic Christianity is worth preserving and what ought to be modified or eliminated. Taylor implies this.

21. Protestant and Catholic modernists were confronted by fundamentalists and integralists. See George Marsden, *Fundamentalism and American Culture: The Shaping of Twentieth Century Evangelicalism, 1870–1925* (New York: Oxford University Press, 1980); and Gabriel Daly, *Transcendence and Immanence: A Study of Catholic Modernism and Integralism* (New York: Oxford University Press, 1980).

22. Surely it was a war—you excommunicate or execute your own

people for treason only in time of war! See Kurtz, *The Politics of Heresy: The Modernist Crisis in Roman Catholicism* (Berkeley: University of California Press, 1986).

23. See Paul W. Witte, *On Common Ground: Protestant and Catholic Evangelicals* (Waco: Word Books, 1975); P. Williamson and Kevin Perrotta, eds., *Christianity Confronts Modernity: A Theological and Pastoral Inquiry by Protestant Evangelicals and Roman Catholics* (Ann Arbor, Mich.: Servant Books, 1981); Reinder Bruinsma, Seventh-Day Adventist Attitudes toward Roman Catholicism, 1844–1965 (Berrien Springs, Mich.: Andrews University Press, n.d.); and Thomas Rauch, "Catholic-Evangelical Relations: Signs of Progress," in *One in Christ* 32/1 (1996): 40–52.

24. Keep a close eye on those "evangelical" Catholics, however. See David O'Brien's *Public Catholicism* (New York: Macmillan, 1989); and Michael Cuneo, "Life Battles: The Rise of Catholic Militancy within the American Pro-Life Movement," in Mary Jo Weaver and R. Scott Appleby, eds., *Being Right: Conservative Catholics in America* (Bloomington: Indiana University Press, 1995), 270–299.

25. Frederick Crowe, *Lonergan* (Collegeville, Minn.: Liturgical Press, 1992); Lonergan, *Insight,* 207–244.

26. Lonergan, *Method in Theology,* xi. Mark Noll and George Marsden among the American evangelical Protestants serve as models of the basic stance of the church toward culture to which Vatican II subscribed, not because they are correct in this or that theory but rather because they are similarly disposed in intellect and feeling. The neo-evangelical journey from a fundamentalist sectarian pose to a constructive and critical engagement of culture parallels that of Catholics in the twentieth century. See Noll's *The Scandal of the Evangelical Mind* (Grand Rapids: W. B. Eerdmans, 1994); and George Marsden, *Reforming Fundamentalism: Fuller Seminary and the New Evangelicalism* (Grand Rapids: W. B. Eerdmans, 1987).

27. Well, almost all—he doesn't cotton to Catholic clerics who think they have a right to dissent in public and especially to organize dissent.

28. See Steven C. Rockefeller, *John Dewey: Religious Faith and Democratic Humanism* (New York: Columbia University Press, 1991). For a comment on Dewey's religious life and his view of religion, see W. Shea, "John Dewey's Spiritual Life." *American Journal of Education* 101/1 (November 1992): 71–81. See also Bruce Kuklick's explanation of Dewey's distancing from his religious affiliation: "In part Dewey was also a man on the make. He knew that systematic theology was no longer a sure route to sucess" (in Michael J. Lacey, ed., *Religion and Twentieth Century American Intellectual Life* [New York: Cambridge University Press, 1989]), 82. Kuklicks *Churchmen and Philosophers: From Jonathan Edwards to John Dewey* (New Haven: Yale University Press, 1985) contains the best statement of the secularizing of American thought. John Patrick Diggins,

however, has a sharper sense of the ironies in this American intellectual and spiritual journey.

29. See Kuklick, *Churchmen and Philosophers*. For Dewey's mature critique of aspects of Enlightenment thought, see *Liberalism and Social Action* (New York: Putnam's Sons, 1935), *Individualism Old and New* (New York: Minton, Balch & Co., 1930) and *Freedom and Culture* (New York: Putnam's Sons, 1939). See also Alan Ryan, *John Dewey and the High Tide of American Liberalism* (New York: W. W. Norton, 1995).

30. For example, see Henry Levinson's evocation of Santayana as a critic of the Enlightenment and a sensitive interpreter of religious life in *Santayana, Pragmatism, and the Spiritual Life* (Chapel Hill: University of North Carolina Press, 1992). Levinson's book is a counter-indication to the claim, perhaps true on the whole, that postmodernists are deaf to religious life and meaning.

31. Philip Selznick, *The Moral Commonwealth: Social Theory and the Promise of Community* (Berkeley: University of California Press, 1992).

32. See W. M. Shea, *The Naturalists and the Supernatural* (Macon, Ga.: Mercer University Press, 1984), for discussions of the theories of religion of four naturalist philosophers: Dewey, Santayana, Woodbridge, and Randall.

33. See David Tracy, *The Analogical Imagination: Christian Theology and the Culture of Pluralism* (New York: Crossroad, 1981).

34. I must enter a tiny reservation about the intimate connection between the gospel and the West's search for universal justice and human rights. While it is so in the West, other forms of Christianity, Western and Eastern, do not seem to show much interest in the search. Although I cannot make a judgment about this matter, I can at least suggest that part of the Western search is rooted in the Greek and Roman philosophical theories and that we may find some of its seeds there.

35. Paul Blanshard, *Communism, Democracy and Catholic Power* (Boston: Beacon Press, 1951); Loraine Boettner, *Roman Catholicism* (Phillipsburg, N.J.: Presbyterian and Reformed Publishing Co., 1962). The latter's sale had reached 138,000 by 1989 and was then in its twenty-seventh printing. It simply extends Reformation judgments of Rome to the American scene before the council. For signs of the postconciliar evangelical shift in attitudes, see David Wells's study of the council: *Revolution in Rome* (Downers Grove, Ill.: Intervarsity Press, 1972).

36. Sidney Hook in *The Quest for Being* (New York: Dell, 1934) and *Pragmatism and the Tragic Sense of Life* (New York: Basic Books, 1974).

37. Mark Noll, "The Rise and Long Life of the Protestant Enlightenment in America" in Shea and Huff, *Knowledge and Belief in America*. See also his *The Scandal of the Evangelical Mind*, in which he reviews the lack of thoeretic engagement with serious epistemological and methodological issues by evangelical Protestants.

38. Patrick Carey, "American Catholicism and the Enlightenment Ethos," in Shea and Huff, *Knowledge and Belief in America*, 125–164. See also David O'Brien, *Public Catholicism*.

39. Shailer Matthews, *The Faith of Modernism* ([1924] New York: AMS Press, 1969). Matthews "moved beyond mediating liberalism, however, by adopting inductive scientific methods as the only means of identifying legitimate values in traditional orthodoxy for his own day. Theology for him did not involve loyalty to earlier formulations because each was relative to its cultural setting." The complexity of the scene is displayed in the comment, "Despite his radical theological conclusions, which abandoned much of traditional Christianity, Matthews remained a staunch supporter of churches" (*Dictionary of American Religious Biography*, ed. H. W. Bowden [Westport, Conn.: Greenwood Press, 1977]), 297–298.

40. Philip Gleason, *Contending with Modernity*, 148–152.

41. The documents can be found in Walter M. Abbott, ed., *The Documents of Vatican II* (New York: Guild Press, 1966).

42. Williams S. Green and Gary Porton, "Religious Resources for Political Culture: The Case of Judaism," in Jacob Neusner, ed., *Religion and the Political Order: Politics in Classical and Contemporary Christianity, Judaism, and Islam* (Atlanta, Ga.: Scholars Press, 1996), p. 110.

43. For a thorough discussion of the questions about academic freedom, see Charles E. Curran, *Catholic Higher Education, Theology, and Academic Freedom* (Notre Dame, Ind.: University of Notre Dame Press, 1990); a more recent article, "The Catholic Identity of Catholic Institutions," is in *Theological Studies* 58/1 (March 1997): 90–108; see also "The Theory and Practice of Academic Freedom in Catholic Higher Education," in Charles E. Curran, ed., *History and Contemporary Issues: Studies in Moral Theology* (New York: Continuum, 1996), 179–200; and most recently, James L. Heft, "Academic Freedom: American and Catholic," in *Origins* (February 18, 1999).

44. "Ex corde ecclesiae" in Alice Gallin, ed., *American Catholic Higher Education: Essential Documents, 1967–1990* (South Bend, Ind.: University of Notre Dame Press, 1992), 415 #6.

45. William P. Leahy, *Adapting to America: Catholics, Jesuits, and Higher Education in the Twentieth Century* (Washington, D.C.: Georgetown University Press, 1991. See also David O'Brien, *From the Heart of the American Church: Catholic Higher Education and American Culture* (Maryknoll, N.Y.: Orbis, 1994); and Joseph A. Komonchak, "The Catholic University in the Church," in John Langan, *Catholic Universities in Church and Society: A Dialogue on Ex Corde Ecclesiae* (Washington, D.C.: Georgetown University Press, 1993), 35–55.

46. Many other related issues weigh upon the administrators and the faculties of Catholic (and other Christian) institutions, among them the

role of ministry, the clarity of mission and its relation to tenure policies, inclusiveness and sharpness of intellectual dialogue, the Catholicism of the professorate and of core programs, the genuineness and depth of scholarship and strength of support for it, university governance and Catholic communitarianism, the honesty and authenticity of the university's relations with the church and its leaders and with the public in their communities and constituencies, and the openness of the universities and colleges to challenges from and participation by the variety of Catholic conservatisms and liberalisms.

47. Gregory Lucey, "The Meaning and Maintenance of Catholicity as a Distinctive Characteristic of American Catholic Higher Education: A Case Study," dissertation, University of Wisconsin, 1978. Margaret Steinfels recently remarked, "I believe we have a decade—ten years—in which this question of identity must be honestly addressed and definitively taken on as a commitment and core project of institutions that hope to remain Catholic"; see "The Catholic Intellectual Tradition," in *Origins* 25 (August 24, 1995): 169–171; and Peter Steinfels, "Catholic Identity: Emerging Consensus," in *Origins* 25 (August 24, 1995): 173–177.

48. For a discussion of the implications of *Ex corde ecclesiae* with regard to the Catholic university and its task of evangelization, see James Heft, and Leo O'Donovan, "A University That Evangelizes: *Ex corde ecclesiae* Six Years Afterwards,: in *Horizons: The Journal of the College Theology Society* 23/1 (Spring 1996): 103–112.

49. "Ex Corde Ecclesiae: An Application to the United States, in *Origins: CNS Documentary Service* 26/24 (November 28, 1996): 381–384.

50. Jacob Neusner, *A Rabbi Talks with Jesus: An Intermillennial, Interfaith Exchange* (New York: Doubleday, 1993).

3

Transcendence and the
Bewilderment of Being Modern

• • •

ROSEMARY LULING HAUGHTON

Reactions after reading and pondering Dr. Taylor's stimulating address reflected the scope of his thought, so that it seemed interestingly possible to respond to it in a number of ways, except that I would end up writing a book rather than an essay. The fact is that "Catholic Modernity" raises questions and concerns with which many people are wrestling, and for that alone we owe Dr. Taylor a debt of gratitude.

However, in time my own response focused on two concepts that seem to me to be significant in the address and to hold a key to others. These concepts are that of a "gospel ethic" and that of "transcendence," with which is linked that of "beyond life." To me, these concepts and the link I perceive between them (as, indeed, does Dr. Taylor) are at the heart of the unease and confusion which many modern Christians feel. The link in the end has to do with myth.

As a background to the whole discussion, I think it is helpful to reflect on the basic problem that anyone deals with in the attempt to conceptualize and communicate changes in theological and philosophical thinking—or rather (and this is the real issue) the changing experiences that challenge us to reexamine old concepts, parameters, and especially *assumptions*—and the whole issue of language.

This has to do with the category of "transcendence," with the "beyond life" that is absent in the embracing high-minded humanism that has (at least arguably) led to the development of what Dr. Taylor calls a "rights culture." It has to do with an unease about a development of the concept of "the gospel ethic," which assumes that it is clear to all what the gospel ethic is, that we know who is the "we" who accept that and know it and therefore don't need to ask.

I am, I suppose, "modern"—in at least some of the senses referred to in Dr. Taylor's address. I feel the appropriate indignation at gross injustice and easily assume that "everyone" agrees with me. But I also notice that the waves of national indignation and generosity evoked by the suffering of refugees or famine victims or oppressed populations are selective. Human rights abuses in Cuba are, for some reason, more reprehensible than the much worse ones present in, for instance, Colombia and (not long ago) El Salvador. Likewise "welfare" provision for the poor was popular in the expanding postwar economy, but in the insecure and frightened nineties it is a luxury "we" can't afford. I find myself wondering if this modernity is a construct created for the comfort of "us" or, alternatively, for the better manipulation of "all thinking people" so that the careful and intelligent exploitation of their needs, fears, and weaknesses can continue invisibly. And that consideration pushes me back to wondering about "transcendence" and "beyond life," which a lot of people talk about, wistfully or enthusiastically, and pursue in all kinds of ways they think they would like to pursue but don't know how to set about it. This is true whether they are religious people or not religious at all. Are we pursuing transcendence (or whatever we choose to call it) because the "materialism" of our culture is so blatant? If so, is that an attempt to escape the recognition of the real nature of what we call materialism?

It is at the point when I am caught in this cat's cradle of questions and catchwords that I want to cut free and get enough distance to be able to see of what that tangle is actually made.

This is where the issue of language has to be confronted. The problem with trying to express modernity—any kind of modernity—is that it inevitably has to struggle to articulate itself in language developed to express something quite different. There is no getting around this, but at least one needs to be aware of it. Any kind of social analysis—and "Catholic modernity" in the sense Dr. Taylor uses the phrase *is* a form of social analysis—has to speak a language that is understandable to people who have learned to consider such analysis as important. So it will have to be expressed, at least initially, in categories developed for the purpose of analyzing something else—Enlightenment philosophy and its attendant socioreligious conclusions, for instance, or the curious, puritan fastidiousness of neo-Thomism, neatly crossing the river by stepping on well-balanced stones without noticing the water.

This is the only way to go, as long as it is understood that what is being said, though with the most meticulous scholarly integrity, is skewed by the torsion of language that is no longer appropriate; it doesn't "fit," rather in the way that translations from languages developed to express the thought categories of extremely different cultures can never be more than approximations. Probably all we can aspire to do is reveal beyond dispute the fact that the old categories no longer work. This is itself a considerable step forward, though not much fun for hardworking pioneers who feel more as if they had strayed through Alice's looking glass and found, after prolonged effort, that they are still in the same place.

Given this awareness of the difficulty of expressing changed experience in categories developed to express quite different ones, we still have to try or else remain stuck forever in the old categories. This is what has happened to the church establishment, even to those members of it—such as, for instance, Bernard Häring—who struggle mightily to appreciate and respond to the moral dilemmas that confront Catholics who want to be faithful to the church without sacrificing their intellectual integrity or common sense.

The question arises, however, as to what I mean by "old" categories. This is a helpful question because an awareness of the history of the development of philosophical (and therefore theological) categories of thought shows us that the ones that tangle us up, and because of which we have to deal with the search for "Catholic modernity," are, in fact, not all that old. It is perhaps because the time periods involved are not enormous—hundreds rather than thousands of years—that it is hard to recognize that the myth within which our philosophies operate has changed. We use the same words and don't notice that they refer to a different story. I shall return to this problem as the key to being "modern."

Our humanistic myth was developed by an extremely elite, class-conscious, and male-dominated scientific and philosophical Enlightenment and deeply tinted by the doctrines of nineteenth-century progress. That humanism is our heritage, and it has great, if equivocal, value, but if we are to make use of that heritage as Christians, then it behooves us to be aware that that tradition developed its own necessary clarifications and categories to explain reality and justify behavior. We need not—indeed, must not—simply use those categories as if they were the only normal tools for interpreting experience.

If we are to consider the rights culture and relate it to a gospel ethic, then we have to recognize that human rights, as we define them, and try to legislate for them are the product of a philosophy that, growing from the Renaissance affirmation of individual human worth, sees humanity as a collection of individuals who are affected by the decisions of governments, whether in their civil or military guise. Margaret Thatcher summed up this view (with her usual assumption that she expressed the only sensible opinion) when she said that "there is no such thing as society," only people. This is the premise of democracy as we understand it. We easily forget that the Greek form of democracy, which we claim as our "model," assumed that a small number of people with votes should make the decisions for all the others, such as women and slaves who had no vote. We assume that a mass of citizens who all have votes will correct that and that the remedy for injustice is to ensure votes for everyone and freedom to use them. We are being forced to recognize the failure of this system to deal with corporate power and the oppression and civil rights abuses to which it leads, but in seeking remedies we are still bound by the individualistic categories of our historical Western heritage.

The categories that confine us are expressions of the Renaissance myth of the individual's power to achieve, to be different, to break free of communal bonds. The corollary to this, in time, was the recognition of rights for the individual. If we are now recognizing the limitations of this myth, that does not mean that we deny the achievements of the human spirit that it made possible—in the arts, science, political theory. We can recognize the myth context of Rousseau and Tom Paine and Robert Owen and others in shaping our rights culture and yet know that the framework they worked in is not adequate to address the "modern" situation.

We are only just beginning to perceive that the Renaissance myth is not an adequate way to respond to such things as ethnic hatred, the lack of accountability of multinational businesses, and the dependence on those of elected government. We have formed our affirmation of human rights, of liberties under the law, entirely in terms of the individual, the "rights of man," and it is true that by doing so we have come a long way, on a path certainly influenced by the notions of the Christian churches about justice. We got a lot of this from "Christendom," which allowed the great jurists of the twelfth century to believe that the law of man could be so shaped as to create a human commonwealth reflective of the kingdom of God. They overestimated the reach of human systems, however idealistic, but then they worked in the context of a society that— even if often enough more in the breach than the observance— assumed that its moral code was universal and could demand of individual holders of power a moral responsibility for those over whom that power was exercised.

It is a source of gratitude for us in the Catholic tradition that theologians and jurists made this effort to shape society according to what they could have thought of as "gospel ethic," though they would not have used that phrase. But the social and moral assumptions within which they operated have evaporated. Instead, we have the long and glorious history of groups of men and women who undertook what they thought of as the real gospel tasks of feeding the hungry, nursing the sick, and teaching the ignorant precisely because the system under which they operated no longer regarded these things as the tasks of society at large, even if it was called Christian. And, as Dr. Taylor points out, great movements of liberation were led by committed Christians who demanded freedom for slaves and reduced hours of work for children in factories. But the rise of the unions, which led to the mass of labor laws designed to protect workers from exploitation, was opposed by many church people, especially Catholics, and has been only partially successful even in Western nations, while the rights of workers employed by transnational corporations in developing countries are virtually nonexistent.

The issue, however, is not so much how successful the efforts to establish universal human rights have been as whether the rights culture, even when it works, has allowed those who affirm it to deny the need for anything more, for the "transcendent" or that which goes "beyond life."

Was the moral impulse that drove the rise in the general affirmation of human rights for all based in a "gospel ethic"? Can we, to prove that connection, read the Gospels through the lenses of an Enlightenment, individualist political philosophy? And do we then feel that this reading is normative, or do we need to ask more difficult questions?

The fact is that we don't really know very clearly (though many have strongly argued opinions) what kind of social ethic Jesus embraced because the writers of the Gospels had their own point of view, which was influenced by the ongoing dialogue with new and old converts to "the Way," by the expectation of imminent *Parousia,* and by the need to establish social acceptability for the new faith in a critical environment.

They, in their own way, were dealing with the shift from a myth grounded in the prophetic tradition of Israel, which assumed an agrarian and basically fairly "egalitarian" (to use a historically quite incongruous word) peasant society as the norm, with local leadership and only functionally centralized power for purposes of war or taxes, to marginalized groups trying to survive spiritually within a dominant, centralized urban culture run by other people. However, even without any great depth of New Testament scholarship, we can get a sense of an understanding of human society and relationship based in that prophetic tradition of Israel that was the context of Jesus' mission. We can also recognize in that context social and political attitudes appropriate to people living on, and by, the land but very concerned about the fragility of their hold on it, since their own traditional peasant way of life and its myth were confused and threatened by the existence of landlords, who owned great estates and employed many landless laborers, and by the Roman system, which controlled both peasants and large landowners. But the vision of Jesus, drawn from the prophets, is that of a peasant society in which the health and survival of the individual depends on a clearly articulated and practiced sense of the moral responsibility of the community for its members. If people are told not to take thought for the morrow because God will feed and clothe them, that makes sense because the community of believers assumes the responsibility, laid on it by God, to look after "the least of my brothers and sisters." The "rights" of the individual are the commands of God because the community is not blessed unless it cares for its members.

This is a vision that operates within the Mosaic vision of a people called to freedom from external domination, guided by leaders who are God's servants and living according to systems of justice that reflect God's order of creation.

This is a far cry from the rights culture, which assumes that the care of the individual can be established by laws quite apart from the moral responsibility of the local community. In such a culture, "charities" are necessary, and campaigns to redress wrongs are necessary because the kind of gospel ethic that lays God's command on each one in the community *as* a community is not accepted. If it were, the "normal" response of a community (of whatever size) to examples of exploitation or gross suffering would be to question not the legal system first (though the communal response naturally translates into enforceable ways to reduce the evil) but the viability of a social structure where this moral imperative doesn't seem to be working. This is the message of the prophets of Israel, who saw poverty and exploitation as the result of sin, denounced people who hoarded wealth or monopolized land, and demanded repentance, which involved drastic redistribution of wealth and just wages.

If we take this as a rough sketch of what we could call a gospel ethic—based on the meager documents available plus good historical research—then we are talking about something very different from a rights culture. The very essence of it is a communal solidarity to which people are called as the condition—better, the *description*—of discipleship. This isn't a question of personal virtue, let alone holiness in the sense we have since given to the word. It is a matter of recognizing the basic truth that for the survival and prosperity of the community people are responsible for one another, and that means everyone: slaves, strangers, criminals, and even women, and that responsibility is the way creation *is*. It is the reign of God because it respects the way God set things up, and *therefore*—as the prophets repeated many times—it leads to health and peace and prosperity.

But this wasn't what Christendom thought of as a gospel ethic. It is true that some Christian teachers picked up the prophetic idea in which Jesus' teaching was grounded. Around 200 C.E., Clement of Alexandria (who is not exactly a good role model in other respects) was aware that "all possessions are by nature unrighteous when we possess them for personal advantage and do not bring them into the common stock for those in need." The prophet Isaiah condemned those who add field to field and house to house (5:8) because they were rejecting the social responsibility that Jesus later affirmed, and John Chrysostom echoed this idea: "I have often laughed while reading documents that say 'that one has ownership of fields and house but another has its use.' For all of us have the use and no one has the ownership."[1] We aren't laughing now; we live by a social ethic that takes that division for granted, though it struggles (feebly) to control the grosser kinds of suffering that it causes.

By the Middle Ages, even that early Christian insight—which was already far from the revolutionary gospel ethic of Jesus—had faded and been replaced by the myth of Christendom, as I mentioned earlier. What is Christendom? From one point of view, it was a powerful myth that shaped Catholic thought roughly from the eighth to the fifteenth century (depending on how you define *Christendom*), during which Catholics assumed that it was possible, right, and "natural" for secular powers to acknowledge the common faith taught in the church and a common moral code developed from it. It was Christendom because Christ ruled it through the pope and bishops, through kings and dukes, and even in independent communes, which accepted that teaching as basic to their laws and policies. (Not all of Europe was feudal, and some theologians thought a republican system more in accord with "natural law" than a monarchical one.) But there was enough left of ancient "tribal" loyalties and of a sense of the obvious need for social solidarity of some kind if the land was to be cared for and people protected in a world where life was very local, indeed, to make Christendom a rough and ready praxis of a gospel ethic. (Again, however, that wasn't a phrase anyone used or thought of. The *Church* developed and enforced the ethic, on the assumption that that was what Jesus had told it to do.) But the Church was inevitably shaped by its historical context and experience, and it developed its moral theology and law out of the accepted practices of Roman and (later) local tribal cultures: so, it also interpreted the gospel moral datum in the light of those experiences, and the ethic it developed was open to a lot of justified barbarity. The Church also, as Dr. Taylor points out, felt itself called to preserve Christendom by any means, including war and brutal heresy hunting. This, together with the rise of the merchant classes, the dominance of the cities, and the emergence of Protestantism, led eventually to the disappearance of Christendom as a serious political project, though it endured as a myth, notably in its Calvinist form and in some Catholic systems such as that of Spain. (Philip II clearly felt called to recreate Christendom, though the conditions that had made such a project seem feasible had long vanished.)

Thus to say that the fullness of the rights culture couldn't have come about under Christendom is to say what is true, but not so much because it pointed to a "weakness" in the Christendom myth as because the kind of conceptualizing that can allow us to use such a phrase as "human rights" was not going on and wouldn't be for a long time. There was still too much of a sense of social coherence, whether in the feudal structure or the later medieval communes and independent cities, for that kind of thinking to occur. Justice for each person was certainly an issue but not human rights in the Enlightenment sense. The rights were primarily those of the community—the church and the secular structures whose job was the common good, in whatever forum was in question.

By the seventeenth century, the economic underpinnings of the "social solidarity" ethic of Christendom had been undermined, and what Christians and notably Catholics developed to replace it was charity. This allowed U.S. representatives at the 1996 World Food Congress in Rome to reject the proposal to declare food a human right. Once justice as solidarity has gone, there is no obligation to feed the hungry. It is certainly a good and necessary thing to do—but it is charity, not justice, and we are a very *charitable* culture. It could be agreed, indeed, that the tremendous popular response to appeals on behalf of suffering are less the result of humanist indoctrination into a rights culture than the result of two centuries of religious indoctrination in charity motivated by compassion as *the* Christian virtue. In a culture in which "justice" means, to most people, the legal system only, this is the most powerful expression of human solidarity that most people can conceive.

And that brings me to the "transcendent" bit. The individualist thinking that made possible the rights culture grew up alongside the individualistic notion of spirituality—spirituality as private, separate from secular life, and expressing itself in prayer and good works. These included some very remarkable "works" that led to the creation of what amounted to whole systems (though they wouldn't have been called that) of education and health care for the poor. The taken-for-granted solidarity of interdependence, as the prophets and Jesus taught it, expressed in terms of justice was no longer part of Catholic spirituality. (I wonder what Jeremiah or Jesus would have made of the idea of "spirituality" as we have come to use it?) This shift, to charity as an expression of personal goodness and compassion based on a love of God cultivated in prayer, went along with the separation of material from spiritual that indeed had existed since the early Middle Ages. The difference was that medieval wealthy people knew that they had better spend a lot of that wealth on things like hospitals and other relief for the needy or risk hellfire (or, at any rate, a very long spell in purgatory) and that "oppression of the poor" was likewise a short route to perdition. You might postpone the reckoning as long as possible, but you had better acknowledge that gospel ethic in practical ways before you died! The devout of the eighteenth or nineteenth century, however, were more likely to think of alleviating the suffering of the poor as a personal response to God's call than as a basic ethical requirement. Such behavior had to do with the demands of the transcendent; it was part of a spiritual perception. It certainly had to do with something beyond the concept of everyday, secular life and material things. There was even an element of guilt: to be too materially comfortable was to be less spiritual, and commitment to the needs of the poor was often a way of escaping from, or compensating for, the comforts and privileges of life. It is still a prominent element in charitable appeals.

This is far from the attitude of the prophets, who saw joyful abundance as the proper result of living according to God's commands. It is also far from the gospel ethic of Jesus as far as we can recover it: he was prepared to embrace hardship and death if his mission required that and to expect similar courage from his disciples, but there is no indication of the self-denial of the later Catholic piety or of guilt about the enjoyment of good things. In that myth, "human flourishing," the "fullness of life," are the will of God, and they *are* life; they are not beyond life, though that life may reach beyond death. Fullness of life is the experience of God, and God's love, God's will, and God's blessing are experienced in material flourishing and in spiritual freedom and holiness—both, and not separately. If the fullness of life is transcendence, then transcendence can be experienced as a good harvest and healthy children.

But to put it like that is to wrench the meaning of the word *transcendence,* which, as a theological term, is part of the dualistic interpretation of reality that separates flesh and spirit, material and spiritual, secular and religious.

Transcendence is opposed to immanence, and Catholic theology, recently, has been haunted by the fear that Catholics would become too concerned with immanence (all this New Age stuff, wisdom theology, and those dangerous feminists!) and lose the transcendent perception of God.

The problem is that the way the word is used does not merely reflect Vatican paranoia about materialism (a paranoia that is, in any case, about a hundred years out of date) but is also used to express the longing for the "something more" that Dr. Taylor refers to. At this point in Catholic history, there is plenty of reaction to the dualistic myth, plenty of emphasis on "life affirming" in Christianity, plenty of rejection of Catholic guilt and gloom about sex, and plenty of attempts to dump original sin, as well as at least some interpretations of the Pauline doctrine of atonement. We have even reached the point where all this life affirming has come to seem, to some of us, a denial of the reality of evil and a simplistic escape from an ancient dilemma. Dr. Taylor is quite right about the pervasive spiritual unease of many who are not content with human flourishing in the humanist version (is it heresy to suggest that life in More's Utopia would be very *boring?*) and have forgotten the prophetic version. It isn't enough, and it is precisely in situations where people are, to a measurable extent, flourishing that the unease and the restlessness and the spiritual searching are most evident.

So there has to be some way to express the longing, the passionate, unquenched desire that so many people experience. We can no longer interpret it easily as, maybe, a religious vocation or a call to personal holiness if that means adding a greater spiritual dimension to one's life. And yet we can't, at this date, immerse ourselves in the collective, the tribal religious impulse—except perhaps in moments of high enthusiasm. Some years ago, I attended the consecration of Bishop Barbara Harris, the first episcopal consecration of a woman in the Anglican communion. Thousands of people filled a huge auditorium because no cathedral was big enough. It was an experience of extraordinary power, of thanksgiving and love and sorrow and hope and grief, and it would be tempting to describe it as a transcendent experience (however paradoxical for a Catholic); yet, I find I can't do that without devaluing the sacramental quality of the more ordinary experiences of shared life.

That is why I find being a modern Catholic bewildering. Modern Catholics (and many other Christians, Jews, and people of other faiths) have tried to capture an integral and nondualistic vision of religion that embraces joy and, indeed, *fun* but that also accepts with enthusiasm necessary discomfort, pain, or worse if that is necessary for the sake of justice—which turns out to mean a way of life formed by an awareness of created interdependence. But we don't have the language, and we are stuck with trying to explain what it is we long for more than we have without using words like *beyond* or *transcendent*. We want that life-affirming prophetic joy, but we also want the stiffening of heroism because the achievement of justice, God's reign—the-way-things-are-meant-to-be—often requires heroism as an ongoing way of life.

I think Dr. Taylor is right when he is grateful and amazed at modern people's capacity for long-distance charity and compassion, even though it may be capricious and too emotionally driven rather than based in the conviction of the primacy of justice. And I share his questions about how the demands for concern on a global scale can be sustained psychologically, socially, economically, or spiritually. (I hate separating those out because they are obviously so closely interrelated, but it is important to realize the scope of the problem that affects all aspects of ourselves, which means our relationships—personal, financial, and political.)

What I am suggesting is that the problem is one of mythmaking. My impression is that Dr. Taylor is trying to correct an inherited myth to fit new needs. Neither the humanist myth nor the Christendom myth fits the experience of a culture in the throes of a transition so rapid and so radical that people snatch at vague contentless concepts like "values" to express the need for some place to stand in the middle of an earthquake.

Ricci, at least, knew his myth thoroughly and thought he could make it intellectually accessible to men of good will in an alien culture who were sufficiently educated and had a kind of leisure of the emotions and the spirit, as well as available time. That kind of thing happens, if it happens, only in a rarefied quasi-academic mode. That isn't our situation. Our myth is no longer coherent, it doesn't offer a story we can live by, and it is challenged not just by polite intellectual exchanges but by brutal and inescapable experience that batters our careers, our families, our world picture, our hopes and expectations.

We long for whatever it is that is represented by words like *transcendent,* and *beyond life,* yet doubt (at least I doubt) that pursuing it in those terms can lead to anything but theological and spiritual dead ends.

In this short essay, I am not about to propose a new myth. That is a project on which many are at work, and I will only mention here Angela Tilby's remarkable book, *Soul: God, Self, and the New Cosmology,* which relates Christian myth to the language of modern physics. The scientific constructs of this century do, indeed, push us to recognize the inadequacy of the conceptual language we inherited from the Renaissance. The recognition of the impossibility of "objectivity" knocks out huge chunks of moral discourse, for instance, and chaos theory marries unpredictability with inherent organization in a way that is causing a revolution in business methods and might give pause to religious ideologies of either left or right. (Those political labels, however, are in themselves discredited as realistic references to actual experience, which is another aspect of the vanishing Enlightenment myth.)

There are other ways of seeking to allow the birth of a different myth, and they are connected to such things as the breakdown in separation between orthodox and alternative methods (in health care, education, farming, and so on), including something like the "thousandth" monkey syndrome. They are all significant. The important thing is that a myth is something that is born of immense numbers of individual and collective experiences that seek expression. The "midwives" can be the insight of significant individuals or the impact of a great event or symbol, the approaching millennium being one of the latter, giving powerful impetus to the struggle to break free of previously accepted categories of thought.

However, it is important for us as Catholics to take an intelligent part in this birthing process. To use the word *intelligent* here may seem odd because the baby is going to be born, no matter how stupid the mother or the others involved. But the baby may be born dead or damaged, or it may be born healthy and lively. A good outcome depends on a lot of cooperation with the process, at the instinctual level certainly, but also through a thorough understanding of what is happening, through good preparation, and through intelligent participation. As modern Catholics, we are in a position to help the process in important, perhaps indispensable ways, and we are not likely to do this if we interpret the event in terms of an outdated clinical picture.

Maybe that is pushing the image too far—but there is some truth there that needs to be considered. The Catholic tradition contains age-old elements that are emerging as part of a new myth. The Catholic notion of sacrament, for instance, in some sense at least, breaks down the transcendent-immanent dichotomy and reestablishes "thingness" as a locus of divinity. (The best exposition of sacramental symbolism that I know of is the story and film *Babette's Feast*.) Embedded in Catholic tradition is a much older tradition of sacredness, in wells, mountains, and caves (as at Lourdes) and in *people*, whose holiness in life imparts a power of holiness to their bodies, even after death.

To make use of such a heritage, to recognize and nurture it in a new form, distinguishing it from what is to be let go, we need to understand at least a little about what myth is.

Libraries have been filled with books about that. For my purposes here, and perhaps for the purposes of many "ordinary" modern Catholics, it is helpful to remember the words of the great mythmaker J. R. R. Tolkien, who was, not incidentally, a lifelong and deeply convinced Catholic. Because he was good at the deliberate creation of a myth for which he saw a need, he knew that the great myths of humankind are not "invented" but birthed—though he would not have used such an image. He *invented* myths because he wanted to share the values of a world he loved whose heritage, he felt, was in danger of being forgotten. It was the world of old England and Norse heroism, whose virtues of courage and endurance were, indeed, allied to those whose absence in the bland humanist vision Dr. Taylor rightly deplores. Because he could invent myths, he knew that myth is never entirely an invention: otherwise, it would not raise profound and even glass-shattering echoes in the minds of the millions for whom humanist flourishing is not enough.

Tolkien knew about myth, and in a conversation with C. S. Lewis, recalled by Tolkien's biographer, Humphrey Carpenter, he spelled out its nature as fundamental to human existence. C. S. Lewis, at the time, had discovered a belief in God but could not cope with Christ and the mythology, as he recognized it, of sacrifice and resurrection. To Lewis, at that point, myths were lies—beautiful and significant but not *true*. Tolkien, in Carpenter's reconstruction of the conversation, replied with an argument about *words*—and the problem of words is, as I suggested earlier, at the heart of our bewilderment as modern Catholics.

> You call a tree a tree, he said, and you think nothing more of the word. But it was not a "tree" until someone gave it that name. You call a star a star, and say it is just a ball of matter moving on a mathematical course. But that is merely how *you* see it. By so naming things and describing them you are only inventing your own terms about them. And just as speech is invention about objects and ideas, so myth is invention about truth.
>
> We have come from God, and inevitably the myths woven by us, though they contain error, will also reflect a splintered fragment of the true light, the eternal truth that is with God. . . . Our myths may be misguided, but they steer however shakily towards the true harbor, while materialistic "progress" leads only to a yawning abyss and the Iron Crown of the power of evil.[2]

Lewis drew from this conversation the perception that the Christ event is *a myth that really happened*, and on that basis he made the step to Christian faith.

From our later perspective, it is possible to notice that Tolkien did not recognize that what he called "materialism" also has its myth, but it seems to me that his words, even now, give us the clarity and encouragement we need. We are telling our stories differently—and the difference is upsetting, but, as Catholics, we may actually discover that the language of an emerging myth is more familiar and more congenial than the secular rights culture, which, when its own myth is undermined by the evidence of human evil and the failure of so many well-meant efforts devised in terms of that myth, finds no firm ground to stand on in the upheaval. My own take on Catholic modernity is that the birthing of a new myth is being greatly assisted by, for instance, new studies of Jesus, some revivals (with a difference) of old devotions, the emergence of women's rituals both fairly orthodox and not so orthodox, and the revived interest in Celtic Christianity, with its uncentralized ecclesial system and ability to absorb and transform pre-Christian myth and ritual.

On the fringes but relevant to the emergence of a new myth (and viewed with intense suspicion by much of the male establishment, both religious and academic) is the patient uncovering of the remains of a culture from the Neolithic to the early Bronze Age, extending across most of Europe and the Near East and culminating in a full-blown civilization in areas of what is now Turkey, with trade routes, town planning, and a developed art but no centralized power, no defensive systems or weapons of war, and no large differences of wealth or prestige, a civilization that lasted altogether from about 7000 B.C.E. to 2800 B.C.E. They worshiped the divine primarily, though not only, in female form and celebrated both birth and death. What was their myth? They used their script only ritually, and it hasn't been deciphered so we don't know, although some of their symbols turned up in Celtic art, including Christian art. But the questioning and the myth exploring goes on, and it is intertwined with the new and old question about the Theotokos, she of the vast mosaics, of the grottoes and springs, of the peasants and the poor, continuing her love-hate relationship with the official church.

The work of modern Catholics is the ongoing redemptive task of naming and telling old stories that, as they are retold, become new. We need not fear being what Tolkien called "misguided." The variety of stories and the mistakes and corrections and repetitions are part of the process. Long ago, there was a sensible man, a member of the religious authority called Gamaliel, whose example could profitably be attended to by other religious authorities. He was confronted with a group of people accused of propagating a new myth. He advised his more punitive colleagues: "Leave them alone. For if this idea of theirs or its execution is of human origin, it will collapse; but if it be from God, you will never be able to pull them down, and risk finding yourselves at war with God."[3]

The emergence of genuine myth is of God, and it emerges from the hearts of many, unlike myths imposed for purposes of dominance. The health and beauty and courage of Catholic myth have always sprung from the hearts of faithful people who are telling and retelling, correcting, elaborating, discerning true from false as time passes, reshaping true and repenting false. From this point of view, Catholic modernity seems both more difficult and much easier, more central to humanity's future and also a lot more fun.

Notes

1. *Concerning the Statues:* Homily 2.18.
2. Humphrey Carpenter, *Tolkien.* (Boston: Houghton Mifflin, 1977), 147.
3. Acts 5:38–39 (my translation).

4

Matteo Ricci and the Prodigal Culture

• • •

GEORGE MARSDEN

Charles Taylor's essay is a model of what scholars who are Christians should be doing. They should be explicitly reflecting on how their faith provides fresh perspectives for viewing contemporary issues. They should be fully engaged with modern scholarship yet be openly critiquing the premises of modernity (which includes "postmodernity") in the light of their Christian commitments.

Because I am in such fundamental agreement with this project and find Taylor's analysis both subtle and insightful, it is not easy to offer a critique. Taylor at least anticipates, even if he may not always answer, many of the potential objections. So even as I raise some critical issues, I do so not primarily to counter what Taylor says but to see if I can suggest some hard questions that may stimulate further refinements.

Taylor's Riccian approach to modernity seems to mean that we should approach modernity on its own terms, as much as it is possible for Catholics and other Christians to do so without vitiating the essentials of our traditions. We should steer between two extremes. Unlike fundamentalists who declare war on modern culture, Christians of traditional commitments should affirm its achievements. At the same time, unlike modernists who, in effect, make modern standards normative and rewrite the traditions accordingly, we should be critical of the inadequacies of modernity. The key to this balance is to focus on synthesizing the best achievements of modernity with authentically Christian traditions.

Taylor nicely illustrates this approach with respect to disestablishment of Christianity in the West. The grand ideal of Christendom was deeply flawed in that it married the teachings of Christ to political coercion. One major accomplishment of modernity was the sundering of this unequal yoke. In effect, it freed the spirit of Christ's teachings of equal regard for all persons from the inevitably exclusivist letter of Christendom's law.

Taylor's Riccian approach involves recognizing the valuable achievements of modernity and using them as the points of contact for presenting the gospel. Particularly, we can see the great good in rights culture, which asserts the claims to equal rights among all peoples. Moreover, Christians can affirm the value of the preeminent goal of that culture, which is to promote human flourishing.

These affirmations, however, carry with them a critique. The most telling part of Taylor's sympathetic critique of modernity's exclusive secularized humanism is that it has no remotely adequate way to deal with death and suffering. If human flourishing is exclusively our goal, then these are simply negatives. Christians, by contrast, can see death and suffering as doors that open us to the knowledge that there is more beyond this life. That insight, moreover, need not undercut our valuing of this life. Rather, it may enhance how we value it.

Taylor moves from this point to an explicit Christian apologetic. Exclusively secular humanism fails in its attempts to provide a coherent basis for affirming the very human values that moderns and postmoderns most strongly affirm. They cannot account for why we should regard all people as inherently equal or why we should limit our own interests by concern for the poor, the weak, or the other. Contemporary ideals ask us to stretch further than ever in embracing peoples all over the world. Yet, if we base our sense of self-worth on such altruism, we are bound to become hopelessly frustrated. Moreover, as has been endlessly illustrated in the twentieth century, a too-great zeal for justice leads to intolerance and injustice.

While rudderless contemporary philosophies flounder among these issues, Christian faith charts a course that at least takes them all into account. To be in the image of God means to stand alongside all others in the stream of God's love. Although the competing philosophies surely fail to generate the love necessary to implement modern ideals, Christianity provides the hope that by being united to the love of God we can at least address these issues. So, we can compare the Christian hypothesis to the hypothesis of a godless universe. Even looking at the question simply in terms of the ideals of human flourishing affirmed by modernity itself, we can challenge our contemporaries: Which hypothesis better accounts for what they wish to affirm?

This all makes good sense to me. Nevertheless, I can suggest a number of issues that may prod Taylor to refine his account and to fill it out more.

To begin with, I wonder whether the Ricci image is the best to employ. It does signal an attitude of leading with our affirmations of modernity rather than with our condemnations. Beyond that, however, as Taylor recognizes, it simply does not work very well because the relationship between Christianity and our culture is so different from that between Christianity and sixteenth-century Chinese culture.

I think the elaboration of another metaphor implicit in Taylor's account may be more helpful for illuminating the complexities of the stance that Christians should take toward modernity. Taylor's main argument can be seen as a proposal for Christianity to reach out to its prodigal offspring (recognizing, of course, that Christianity was not modernity's only progenitor). This prodigal is immensely attractive and has many genuine accomplishments that Christians should admire. Some of these accomplishments are wonderful applications of Christian principles that were taught, even if seldom put into practice, when everyone lived at home. Still the prodigal's principles are deeply flawed and dangerous, not least of all to the prodigal, who has been living high on borrowed moral and intellectual capital much longer than anyone has the right to expect. Disillusion and cynicism can be temporarily avoided only by the distractions of material pleasures and self-indulgence. None of these can make any sense of a person's inevitable suffering and death. Yet, through it all, through all the self-contradictions, the prodigal remains a person of high ideals. These ideals, which resonate with some primitive Christian teaching, provide a point of contact. Christians must show the prodigal that the only realistic hope for realizing these ideals is by coming home.

The metaphor of the prodigal works better than that of Matteo Ricci's mission because it better resolves some of the problems, which Taylor recognizes, of viewing modern secular humanism as though it were a wholly foreign culture. It also gives a fuller account of why we should admire many of the achievements of secularism. It suggests that our affirmation of what is good in modernity is more than an effective accommodationist missionary strategy. Further, the analogy to the prodigal also implies an appreciation of modernity that is based on more than the theological point that God's grace may be seen operating in cultures that have been beyond the bounds of explicit gospel proclamation. Rather, it focuses on and vivifies Taylor's point that there is a partial Christian lineage behind the accomplishments of modernity. This family tie provides a basis for a genuinely loving sympathy, without which we will always be talking past one another. The loving father is going to give the benefit of the doubt to the prodigal.

The image of the prodigal helps clarify another dimension that I think is faithful to what Taylor intends to say. It highlights the deep ambivalence that Christians should have toward modernity. It is not just non-Christian. It is, in part, an anti-Christian rebellion, with all the bitterness that a broken family relationship can engender. Ultimately, it is a rebellion not only against Christianity but also against God's love (even if institutional Christianity often must share the blame for keeping people from seeing God's love). It is, moreover, a rebellion that takes God's gifts that are potentially good and turns them to evil by absolutizing them. In Augustinian terms, it is a rebellion of directing one's most impassioned love toward some limited aspect of creation rather than to the Creator. Such misplaced love is ultimately destructive both of self and of the ability to love others.

Taylor, in his Riccian mode, does not say anything about rebellion and sin, although it is implicit in his account. He is probably right that talking about sin is not the best place to start our Christian witness to the more progressive of our contemporaries. Letters to alienated children that condemn everything in their lifestyle are going to get tossed away in anger. Better to sympathetically consider their interests and aspirations in their own terms and gently lead them to see their emptiness. Taylor's best-known work, *Sources of the Self*, might be seen as exemplifying the approach he here suggests. *Sources* is an extended essay on the particular genius of modern sinfulness, but it may have alienated many potential readers to make explicit Christian teaching integral to the story.

Then again, it is worth asking whether we have to be so shy of the particularities of Christian doctrines. Like Ricci dressing as a Confucian scholar, do we always have to dress our views in terms already acceptable to the contemporary academy? Reinhold Niebuhr, after all, talked openly of the biblical teaching of "original sin" and found a wide hearing, even among some of the atheists of his generation. Unfortunately, he was sufficiently vague on most other Christian teaching that he now appears to many to have been essentially a Protestant liberal, even if a chastened one. Nonetheless, the point remains that some modern people might recognize an answer to their questions in the particularities of Christian accounts of things. We do not need to start with those issues that will heighten the alienation, but eventually and tactfully we should get to them. To put it another way, we need to recognize that ultimately the gospel claims are an "offense," even if we have to be careful not to add to that offensiveness in the way we present them.

How Christian scholars may handle these issues is, as the Riccian model suggests, partly a matter of strategy. One way is to speak differently to different audiences, as Taylor seems to. So in *Sources of the Self* the form is that of a detached modern treatise in which "we" look together at the peculiarities and the problems of modernity. The substance, however, is clearly controlled by questions shaped by a Christian agenda, and few clues are provided to allow the reader to surmise that is what is going on. At least one can tell that the agenda is Judeo-Christian and theistic. Only the most acute readers might surmise that the author is Catholic, if they did not know that already. "A Catholic Modernity?" by contrast, is addressed first of all to a Catholic academic audience, and the "we" refers to Catholics who face the question of how to speak to the modern world. Perhaps still in deference to academic conventions, it tiptoes around some of the theological issues, but in at least one crucial point it is explicitly Trinitarian. Presumably in a nonacademic church or private setting, Taylor would elaborate on such theological points.

I find Taylor's approach sensible and attractive. It is far superior to the approach of many scholars who are Christian. The usual conventions for most scholars who are religious is that they should view their scholarship as "public" and their faith as "private" and do the best they can to keep these two domains separate. Although their Christian commitments may inevitably have some impact on their scholarship, they seldom think about that impact or make any effort to develop its implications. They do not, as Taylor does, challenge contemporary assumptions with penetrating questions that are self-consciously controlled by their religious commitments. Whether they are in secular or church-related academic settings, they think that their professional duty is to separate faith from learning so far as is possible. They may talk privately about their faith or talk about theology in Sunday school, but they do not see these very large claims about reality as having any bearing on their public or professional academic lives.

So Taylor's work is an alternative model that should be emulated. Today, there are a number of such models, although most of them seem to be in the field of philosophy. Unlike most other fields, a substantial part of philosophy's professional heritage deals with questions of faith and learning. Moreover, philosophers have to pay attention to good arguments about first principles. Practitioners in other fields typically take their first principles for granted. Taylor's work, which delves into the vast realms of history and culture studies, should be a model for scholars in other fields.

Nonetheless (because Taylor raises the question of Christian strategy in evoking the Riccian model), I wonder if more should not be done. In this day of "diversity" and recognition of the salience of "social location," do we have to tiptoe around our Christian commitments so much in our professional work? For instance, near the end of *Sources of the Self*, Taylor says the following.

> I am obviously not neutral in posing these questions. Even though I have refrained (partly out of delicacy, but largely out of lack of arguments) from answering them, the reader suspects that my hunch lies towards the affirmative, that I do think naturalist humanism defective in these respects—or, perhaps better put, that great as the power of the naturalist sources might be, the potential of a certain theistic perspective is incomparably greater.[1]

As much as I admire tact and modesty, I wonder if *Sources* would not be a more complete, well-rounded, and effective book if it included something like the present essay as its conclusion. I realize that one is almost always on firmer ground in exposing the weaknesses of other positions than in convincing people of the potentialities of one's own. Yet, Taylor clearly *is* capable of producing some good arguments for his view, and *Sources* might have been a considerably more *Christian* tour de force had he spelled out his position and argued for its superiority. Taylor mentions that he thinks it might be indelicate to do so, but I wonder if that is not deferring too much to the hegemony of the very naturalistic standards he seeks to challenge. It is, after all, possible to argue firmly for one's position yet do it with tact and modesty. And, as Alasdair MacIntyre exemplifies, it is not true that philosophers' arguments will be dismissed if they speak out for a Christian alternative.

One reason that we might consider not so often dressing like the secular humanists in our professional scholarship is that they are not the only "moderns" with whom we are dealing, even in the academy. They may seem to be the only party, but that is because our academic conventions favor an exclusively naturalistic discourse, even for those who are not themselves exclusively naturalistic. In fact, contrary to the way we academics usually speak about it, modernity involves a lot of traditional religious belief and believers. This is especially true in North America. For instance, two-thirds of Canadians say they "believe that Jesus Christ was crucified, died and was buried, but was resurrected to eternal life." Almost as many affirm that Jesus' life, death, and resurrection provided a way for their forgiveness.[2] Even taking into account that polling data tend to yield inflated claims of religious belief, even if only half were at all serious about these beliefs, we are talking about a very sizable portion of the population. Many of them must be attending colleges and universities, and a fair number must be teaching in them as well. Many people would never know it, however, because our academic culture teaches us self-censorship of our religiously informed views.

This point is crucial for considering strategy because the hard-line secularists are not the people that we are likely to convince through the excellence of our Christian scholarship or by comparing our hypothesis to theirs. Faced with good arguments, dedicated secularists will, in all likelihood, react like most strongly committed people and harden their intellectual defenses around what they already believe, particularly if they perceive politicized behavioral issues centering around sexuality to be at stake.

The people whom Christian academics are far more likely to reach are the large mass of people who stand somewhere in the middle. For them, modernity involves a struggle between religious traditions and secularism. Many believers have little guidance on how to deal with the many negotiations demanded by juxtapositions of the contradictory traditions that have shaped them. Many others are nominal believers who affirm traditional Christian doctrines if asked by a pollster but live essentially secular lives. All these are people for whom articulate Christians in the academic mainstream may be an immense help. These people will not be facing the question of "their hypothesis versus mine." Rather, questions for them will be, Which of these two hypotheses, each of which I find to be a live option, should I affirm? Which of the traditions of which I find myself a part best accounts for who I am, what I need, and what ideals I should affirm? For such people in the middle, the articulate Christian academic can be an invaluable model and guide.

We must keep in mind, of course, that arguments are not the only things that win arguments. When traditions clash, we are dealing with contests between communities and ways of life. Christians who are scholars also need to be parts of Christian communities. They also need to build subcommunities, centers, and networks with other Christian scholars and to cultivate Christian spirituality and virtues. Here may be another reason to think twice about the Riccian approach. There is a danger that our identification with modern academia may become our primary identification. Because people are socialized and shaped by their closest associates, it is important for Christian scholars to be participating in Christian communities and cultivating subcommunities of Christian scholars. Thomas Kuhn points out that the way people are converted from one paradigm to another is not so much by arguments as by observing the fruitful problem-solving of another community. "They say: I don't know how the proponents of the new view succeed, but I must learn whatever they are doing, it is clearly right."[3] Good arguments are essential to the Christian case, especially for clearing away the impression that such arguments do not exist, but ultimately the case must be made by example as well.

A number of other strategic considerations have to be taken into account in implementing this suggestion that more Christians in the academic mainstream should be openly engaging in the hard work of relating their faith to their learning. First, it is important to emphasize that what applies to Christians applies to other faith traditions. Many Jews and Muslims, for instance, are likewise caught between theistic traditions and naturalistic humanism and need scholars to lead them through the maze of the religious-secular dilemmas of modernity. They, too, should be encouraged to articulate the implications of their faiths within the academic mainstream. So this proposal is not to reestablish Christian hegemony in mainstream culture but to make an irreversibly pluralistic academic culture more genuinely pluralistic by including religious perspectives.

Second, it is often easier for senior academics who are recognized in their fields to take off the secular humanist garb than for younger and less established scholars to do so. In that sense, the Riccian strategy may still be requisite for those entering a field and looking for jobs and tenure. Changing the conventions of academic culture is not easily done, and old prejudices against religious beliefs remain strong. Nonetheless, senior scholars can be setting examples and mentoring junior scholars so that eventually the conventions will change.

A third point to recognize is that it is easier and more appropriate to articulate the implications of one's faith in some fields than in others. In more technical parts of disciplines and in disciplines that are mostly technical, religious faith may not seem to make much difference. But as soon as a discipline touches on wider questions of meaning, faith may have an important bearing. This will be more often the case for philosophers than for physicists. Yet, as we all know, once they have won a Nobel Prize, physicists often turn into metaphysicians.

With a being as great as God as a serious part of our intellectual picture, other things in the picture are bound to change. At the least, the relative importance of the rest of the picture will change. This is particularly significant in disciplines that deal with human culture and behavior. Christians and other religiously informed thinkers may find themselves rejecting academic theories that have had immense influence in shaping these disciplines. For instance, they may dissent from the view that human cultural or moral systems are best understood as *exclusively* the result of social evolutionary forces that can be evaluated only on naturalist terms, or they may reject widely current academic views that, in effect, posit that humans are the only creators of "reality." Christian academics would present their critiques of such theories, as Taylor does, on grounds accessible to evaluation by other academics (rather than trying to settle the case by appeals to revealed authority). They would also be open about how their own theistic commitments suggest the hypothesis for which they argue.

These latter points may have a bearing on how one argues concerning the main points made in "A Catholic Modernity?" Taylor is right to begin with an emphasis on looking for the good that the rights culture of modernity has produced. At the same time, it is important to be clear that with God in the picture the goal of promoting "human flourishing" with the widest possible equity is going to look very different than if God is out of the picture. In the latter case, such human flourishing is the supreme goal. All else must be judged by whether it advances this goal, conceived in purely secular terms. Taylor is, I think, clear enough about this point in his own mind because he points out some of the changes in what human flourishing means in a theistic context. Nevertheless, there is a danger in letting modernity set the standards that Christianity must meet if it is to gain credibility. Taylor himself explicitly warns against the trap involved. He is not proposing "a modern Catholicism," in which modernity becomes the standard for repudiating those parts of the tradition that do not suit current tastes. Yet, so many Christian traditions have fallen into that trap that it is worth underscoring that the project of meeting modernity on its own terms often misleads people into letting modernity set the standards. People need to be reminded that theistic and nontheistic humanism are ultimately not the same.

Taylor himself, however, does keep his theism in view and uses it ultimately to challenge people to see that their goals of human flourishing are empty and unobtainable without it. Though he keeps explicit theological statements to a minimum, he does state the crucial point in encapsulated form. Our being "in the image of God," he says, means that we are accepted in God's love unconditionally, not on the basis of what we have made ourselves. Moreover, this acceptance is not an individualistic thing, "me and God," as so much of contemporary piety would suggest. Rather, "Our being in the image of God is also our standing among others in the stream of love, which is the facet of God's life we try to grasp, very inadequately, in speaking of the Trinity." Here is the vision of reality that the prodigals or potential prodigals of modernity must grasp if they are to be brought to the home where they can truly flourish. Ultimately, this vision points, as the allusion to the Trinity suggests, to God's own Son, who bore the weight of our rebelling. Glimpsing such sacrificial love and being overwhelmed by the power of its beauty can, indeed, draw us into a stream of love that is our only hope and comfort in life and in death.

Notes

1. Charles Taylor, *Sources of the Self: The Making of modern Identity* (Cambridge: Harvard University Press, 1989), 517–518.

2. This is based on the 1983 "Religion Poll" conducted by the Angus Reid Group and George Rawlyk, as reported in *Macleans,* April 12, 1993, pp. 32–50. Comparable polls of professions of religious belief in the United States always show even higher levels of traditional belief.

3. Thomas S. Kuhn, *The Structure of Scientific Revolutions,* 2nd ed. (Chicago: University of Chicago Press, 1970 [1962]), 203.

5

Augustine and Diversity

• • •

JEAN BETHKE ELSHTAIN

"Human diversity is part of the way we are made in the image of God," Charles Taylor writes. This understanding of diversity affords a complex and capacious view of the human condition. Our differences are not so radical that we are doomed to be forever strangers, alienated from one another. At the same time, our commonalities are not so transparent and irresistible that we are slated for a world of strong unity bordering on homogeneity. No, matters are far more nuanced, as is the Trinitarian God: three in one, one in three, coequal yet distinct, never separate but always differentiated, never solidified but always united. There is no easy way to construe diversity as an analogue or reflection of the *imago Dei*. And why should there be? Our early Christian forebears struggled with and against one another long and hard as they hammered out the Trinitarian doctrine, as they wrote the creed we recite, and as they recalled the story of human beginnings as captured by St. Augustine: *Initium ut esset homo creatus est*—that a beginning be made, man was created.

I want to deepen Taylor's claim that a recognition of human diversity is what you derive if you ponder what it means to be made in the image of God. We are bombarded daily with the message of diversity. It is a code word and a passkey. Diversity has become an end unto itself. We see ourselves as different, and we declare difference good. Those who raise questions about how diversity at present has been defined and politicized are often accused of not being able to "deal with diversity" or of "hating the Other" or of wanting to shove "the different" out of sight and out of mind. If you aren't *for* diversity, the argument goes, you must be for homogeneity and "normalizing" all human materials into an undifferentiated mass under the hegemonic control of the culturally dominant. There are even those in our academies and polities who turn difference or diversity into incommensurability: if I am white and you are black, I can't "get it" by definition. Similarly, if I am female and you are male, we are bound to stare uncomprehendingly at one another from across an abyss.

This sort of thing can go on endlessly. The upshot, if the incommensurability argument is pushed hard enough, is the insistence that we inhabit something akin to radically alien social and mental universes, that there are no terms of commonality that help us bridge differences, and that it is *only* with those who are different *just like us* that communication and even the most rudimentary forms of living together are possible. Human dialogue, it follows, is impossible under such circumstances. As Albert Camus once remarked: "For dialogue, we have substituted the communiqué." The world of radical incommensurable diversity is a world of manifestos and communiqués. It is a world of permanent estrangements. It is a world that obliterates individuality—as I merge with others who are different just like me—even as it prohibits commonality. This is *not* a world in which being made in the image of God is lifted up; rather, if Taylor is right, it is a world in which the *imago Dei* is consigned to the conceptual scrap heap as so much debris labeled "Western metaphysics," "Western logocentrism," "patriarchal hegemony," or a combination of all of these. The hermeneutics of suspicion fuel an absolutist and totalizing project (or may and often do) that involves the utter and complete rejection of transcendence, another theme on which Taylor has written wisely and well.

But I want to keep my eyes on the ball and ask what difference it makes if we resituate human diversity within the *imago Dei*, thereby removing that concern from the rigidly ideological framework in which it is frequently lodged. In other words, what does it mean to be created in God's image?

For help in unpacking this matter, I will turn to Augustine's great work on the Trinity.[1] Augustine helps us see the way in which the *imago Dei* maps onto mind, body, and self with profound implications for our thinking about human diversity and social life. Thinking with and through the Trinity permits us to understand why we are unable to express ourselves transparently and get others to respond to us completely. It enables us to seek the saving grace of our fellow human beings through the transformative and constitutive force of love, *caritas*.

The argument works like this. Being the sorts of creatures that we are, we see the world through forms or conceptual spectacles. As beings circumscribed by bounds of time and space, we require certain fundamental categories to *see* the world at all. Form, which circumscribes, is also a presupposition of human freedom, necessary to our very ability to reason things through. The *primary* form, for Augustine, is the form and form-giving category we call the Trinity, "a principle capable of saving the reason as well as the will, and thus redeeming human personality as a whole."[2] Immersed in time and space, with no possibility of escape, authentic knowledge should chasten rather than inflate us. Working dialogically and analogically, Augustine maps Trinity to mind, mind to Trinity. He at least partially dethrones knowledge (or the Platonic view) in favor of love.

Love may not be all that we need. But love opens up the possibility of coming to know and to appreciate the other. Mind is embodied; body is thought. That form called Trinity is accessible to us in part because it can be represented and experienced immanently—we all have the experience of relations between distinct parts that constitute a whole—in and through our ensouled bodies. Trinity provides food for thought; it occasions a kind of epistemic urgency. This form helps us to seek, to know, to find, by generating the seeking that culminates in community and companionship, a search that must first acknowledge the reality of some other, anticipate the commonalities that draw us together, and engage the differences that separate us yet goad us to friendship and to dialogue. Charity—*caritas*—unlocks our hearts to this possibility.

Our language offers us "probable arguments" for that form we call Trinity, the form in which we are made. As speaking beings, we know that language both unites and divides. Through language, we try to approach God. His hiddenness stymies us. But he is apprehensible through a mediator. God comes down to us so that we might ascend to him. In this way, Trinity is an occasion for complex thought. We are utterly powerless to convey with any completeness the ineffability of God. Much remains mysterious. Just so. Similarly, we cannot pin down all of human reality, including that reality we call a human being, through language. Yet without language we cannot and could not approach one another, much less come toward one another yearning for dialogue and sociability. When we gaze upon things in the mind, then, it is always through a complex word-name-image nexus. We come to see Trinity through imagining, through naming, and through love, and this love provides the horizon for our account of selfhood. In yearning for God, in turning our wills in that direction, in loving God, we also love our neighbor.

Being made in God's image requires, for Augustine, a brake on our own quest for mastery and appropriation. Absolute ownership, exploitation, and domination are forms of being that deny what it means to be formed in and through Trinity. Such forms diminish and amputate rather than enrich, expand, or help to make whole. Making whole means honoring the integrity of each distinct being—distinct, not separate, and certainly not absolute unto itself. Like God, we must empty ourselves so that others might help to fill us. The central symbol of this process of humbling is, of course, the Cross. Only through such a rough symbol, only in homely garb scorned by the world, can we finally submit ourselves to truth by becoming participants in the form in which we are made. The implication here is dramatic and simple, if I have understood Augustine correctly: if we presume that we are the sole and only ground of our own being, we deny our dependence on others, beginning with that Other who made us in his own image. That denial, in turn, invites a refusal of authentic companionship; it spurns the premise and promise of Trinity, of one and many, distinct yet together.

This shifts us to a concern with human plurality, or what Taylor calls diversity. The way Augustine works this out is intriguing. He precisely reverses the motto on all legal U.S. tender: "Out of many, one." For Augustine, it is, rather, "Out of one, many." God did not begin with the human species in the story of creation but with singularity. Other species God commanded to come into being "all at once."[3] But not so the human person. Here God created "one individual; but that did not mean that he was to remain alone, bereft of human society. God's intention was that in this way the unity of human society and the bonds of human sympathy be more emphatically brought home to man, if men were bound together not merely by likeness in nature but also by a feeling of kinship."[4] What's important about this starting point, as Augustine explains in *The City of God*, is that God's purpose is that "the human race should not merely be united in a society by natural likeness but should also be bound together by 'the bond of peace.'"[5] Spread out on the face of the earth, living under many customs, and distinguished by a "complex variety of languages, arms, and dress,"[6] all human beings participate in that fellowship we call human society; all are marked by the point of origin from one; all are called to membership in the earthly society and the city of God.

Even as we learn about mind, self, and other through that form in whose likeness we are made, so we learn about neighborliness and reciprocity by reflecting on our beginnings. This reflection tells us that we are radically incomplete. We cannot "combine many relationships" in one single self; rather, our "connections should be separated and spread among individuals, and that in this way they should help to bind social life more effectively by involving in their plurality a plurality of persons. . . . Thus affection stretches over a greater number."[7] The social tie radiates out from kinship groups to ever-widening circles of sociability; near and far, distant and intimate. There is something mysterious about all this, about what Augustine calls an "inherent sense of decency." Any society that loses this sense of decency is a society in very big trouble, indeed. It is a society that has repudiated, whether tacitly or explicitly, the ground of human *being* and of human *beings-among-others*.

The generosity of Augustine's account is reminiscent of Taylor's, managing to be at the same time realistic and hopeful about our prospects. Rather than an occasion for fear and loathing, our distinctiveness and difference present an occasion for a call to fellowship through a principle of charitable interpretation that helps us to see, to hear, and to understand others, even as they, in turn, can draw closer to us—closer but not to the point that all difference is effaced and all distinctiveness obliterated. As the circles widen, variety increases. The proliferation of varied forms helps us to "compensate for our own narrowness," writes Taylor; it reminds "us of all that we need to complement our own partiality."

And this is the only route to wholeness consistent with being made in the image of God. It is a way that is wary of "triumphalism and self-sufficiency."

The importance of plurality is central for Taylor, as it was for Augustine. Being created in God's image "from one" structures a fragile but real ontology of peace, or anticipated and relative peacefulness. Bonds of affection tie human beings from the start. Bonds of kinship bind us further. The more human relationships are dispersed, finally encompassing the entire globe, and in light of the confounding of human languages, the more difficult it is to repair to this fundamental kinship or sociality. Yet, that's when it becomes especially important. Remember, this is no blanket assertion that "we are all alike." Augustine knew better; Taylor knows better. We are very far apart, indeed. Augustine, the reader may recall, claims that it is easier to have fellowship with one's dog than with a human being speaking a foreign tongue. Nevertheless, there is something like a common nature—in God's image—and this thread of commonality supports both individuality and plurality, helps to constitute us as individuals, and helps to preserve the space between us—out of one, many ones, each a new beginning—yet these many ones share a nature in common.

Here Augustine must be cited at some length.

> Could anyone fail to see, on rational consideration, how marvelous it is that, despite the countless numbers of mankind, and despite the great similarity among men through their possession of a common nature, each individual has his own unique individual appearance? The truth is that if there were not this underlying similarity man could not be distinguished as a separate species from the other animals, while at the same time, without those individual differences, one man could not be distinguished from another. Thus we acknowledge that men are alike, and equally we discover that they are different. Now it is the observation of the differences between men that should arouse our wonder; for the likeness would seem to be normal, as something demanded by our common nature. And yet because it is rarities that rouse wonder, we are much more astonished when we find two people so alike that we are always, or very frequently, making mistakes when we try to distinguish them.[8]

This is a preachment of good sense—and I am also always struck, reading Taylor, by what decent, good sense he makes—especially so in light of the passions of our moment when we are enjoined to homogenize difference on the basis of racial, gender, or ethnic criteria, yet, at the same time, urged to resist with all our might any commonalities, principles, or categories that might help us arrive at common understandings despite disparate experiences. Are we in danger of losing what a "Catholic modernity" might offer us—a via media between denying differences or absolutizing them definitively, between presuming a too thoroughgoing unanimity and negating the possibility of any commonality?

The complex texture of a world constituted in and through the Trinitarian *imago Dei* is what I fear we are in danger of losing. On this score, Taylor may be more hopeful than I. I may be more of a "knocker" than he is, in other words. But, with him, I hope that our capacity to acknowledge and to conceive limits and our yearning for meaning and sociability do not atrophy further but, rather, enjoy a revivification in the next century. Were I to tease a restorative or constructive project out of Taylor's essay, it would begin with a commitment to the dignity of the human person, to democracy under law, and to traditions of political and religious faith in a world in which these are often under direct assault or are being undermined in ways that are subtle and difficult to discern. As well, we are enjoined to repudiate a particular type of human deformation Augustine called "pridefulness," the making of our selves into an absolute principle—the principle of the Selfsame, Augustine calls it. And many forms of contemporary politics become intelligible only if one appreciates that they involve a determination to be the origin of oneself rather than to acknowledge one's incompleteness. The Selfsame, Augustine insisted, is God's alone: the same yesterday, today, and tomorrow. But if we embrace an anthropocentric presumption of the Selfsame, no openhearted action or loving dialogue can come. No, the fruits will be the insistencies of a clamorous, triumphalist self, full of demands, shorn of pity, incapable of critical self-examination.

False pride leads us into all manner of denials. We deny our birth from the body of a woman. We deny our dependence on her and others to nurture and tend us. We deny our dependence on family and friends to sustain us. We most certainly deny that the nations are under God's judgment. Pridefulness denies our multiple and manifold interdependencies and points of mutual recognition. It presumes that we can live on our own resources exclusively. But, as Augustine pointed out, every "proud man heeds himself, and he who pleases himself seems great to himself. But he who pleases himself pleases a fool, for he is a fool when he is pleasing to himself."[9] In late modernity, it is a great temptation to be a self-pleaser. It is a great challenge to embrace the terms of a Catholic modernity, shorn of triumphalism, called to solidarity and to hope, driven by a recognition of our incompleteness and the joy of fellowship. In Taylor's words: "That's because being made in the image of God, as a feature of each human being, is not something that can be characterized just by reference to this being alone. Our being in the image of God is also our standing among others in the stream of love, which is that facet of God's life we try to grasp, very inadequately, in speaking of the Trinity."

In "A Catholic Modernity?" as in all his writings, Charles Taylor models what he calls for: charity and clarity in interpretation, recognition of a human fellowship that honors particular cultures and countries but urges us to cross borders as peaceful pilgrims, the possibility of authentic dialogue by contrast to the clamor of those who demand that we interrogate the past relentlessly, as if we were judges and executioners putting everybody and everything through the third degree, sledgehammer in hand, ready to smash to bits all that has gone before. Not so Taylor. In opening up a dialogue with the dead, Taylor helps us to think about what it means to be "truly alive" in the present. We are in his debt.

Notes

1. Augustine, *The Trinity* (Washington, D.C.: Catholic University of America Press, 1992). I will also draw on my discussion, "Against the Pridefulness of Philosophy," chapter 3 of *Augustine and the Limits of Politics* (Notre Dame, Ind.: Notre Dame University Press, 1995).

2. See Charles Norris Cochrane's discussion in *Christianity and Classical Culture* (New York: Galaxy, 1959), 384.

3. Here I am drawing on Augustine, *The City of Gold* (New York: Penguin, 1985), book XII, chap. 22, p. 502.

4. Ibid.

5. Ibid., book XIV, chap. 1, p. 547.

6. Ibid.

7. Ibid., book CV, chap. 15, p. 623.

8. Ibid., book XXI, chap. 8, pp. 981–982.

9. Augustine, "Psalm 122: God Is True Wealth," in *Selected Writings: Homilies on the Psalms* (New York: Paulist Press, 1984) p. 250.

6

Concluding Reflections and Comments

• • •

CHARLES TAYLOR

I

These four papers set me thinking and reawaken the sense of doubt and uncertainty with which I wrote "A Catholic Modernity?" Rosemary Luling Haughton has captured it so clearly: the words just aren't adequate for what has to be said. You struggle, then put down one term, then erase it impatiently, and try another, and another. And then sometimes you end up using the first one, reinscribing it with a sense of defeat on the grounds that it's not as catastrophically misleading as its rivals.

Reading her, I feel this again about "transcendent." How could I ever have used such an abstract and evasive term, one so redolent of the flat and content-free modes of spirituality we can get maneuvered into in the attempt to accommodate both modern reason and the promptings of the heart? I remember erasing it with particular gusto. Why ever did I reinstate it? What pressures led in the end to its grudging rehabilitation?

Well, one was that I wanted to say something general, something not just about Christians. In the end, I think there is a point one could make about the insufficiency of human flourishing as the unique focus of our lives, which recurs throughout all of human history and cultures, albeit in very different ways. In this sense, there is something unique in our modern "secular," Western culture, in that it is the site of the only large-scale attempt in human history at living an exclusive humanism. The self-congratulatory discourse about our exceptional status on this score is right in this respect: no one else ever tried it. And by virtue of living through this experiment, we will be in a better position to understand why. I needed a term to talk about all those different ways in which religious discourse and practice went beyond the exclusively human, and in exhaustion I fell back on "transcendent." (But I haven't given up hope of finding a better term.)

But then why did I want to say something general? Isn't the subject of discussion Catholics in modernity—that is, us now? Why look abroad?

The answer is that I felt (feel) the need to take a distance, to open out the range of possibilities. I think we are too close or perhaps, rather, both too close and too far from our society to think fruitfully about it.

This was the point of my conceit of a Ricci voyage. Interestingly, George Marsden picked up another facet of this: Ricci's attempts to "go native," not to open up to his interlocutors first and foremost with critique but with an appreciation of what was great in their civilization. That must have been somewhere in my mind, but the principal thing I was thinking of was getting the right kind of distance. It's related to the discussion about two takes on modernity, which William M. Shea refers to.

From within Western modernity, we have a tendency to see it in terms of what it has done away with. Modernity comes with the destruction of traditional horizons, of belief in the sacred, of old notions of hierarchy; it comes with the disenchantment of the world. What all these and similar descriptions have in common is that they characterize modern civilization by what it has set aside. Strangely enough, this kind of take is shared between the most gung-ho "boosters" of modernity, for whom the change is a liberation, and the most inveterate "knockers," for whom it is a loss of the horizons essential to civility, or community, or moral behavior, and the like.

I have called this the "view from Dover Beach," after Arnold's great poem about the ebbing tide of faith. It makes us see modernity as traditional society, minus something, whether this is good riddance or a catastrophic loss. Now from within the polemical stance that it's hard not to assume, be it with boosters or knockers, this way of thinking comes naturally. But I think it obscures a great deal of what is essential and important about our age, things like the affirmation of ordinary life, the new forms of inwardness, and the "rights culture," among others.

These heave into view if we try to stand back from the controversy and approach this civilization as we would if we really came from outside, without preconceptions, and allowed ourselves to be both enthused and horrified by its different facets. This is the kind of distance the Ricci image is meant to win for us.

But I still haven't expressed the whole point. As it stands, it sounds paradoxical. We are too close to our age—in particular, to the polemics that resound through it—and this means that we describe it as its "traditional" predecessor minus something. In short, being too close means we take a detour to describe our age in terms of what it is not. So we have to take a kind of Ricci-distance to get close to it in the proper way. But, of course, that doesn't mean that we are finally focusing just on this age, without reference to any others. The Ricci voyager carries the point of comparison within himself.

And this is inevitable. We always understand something through something else, and, for us, this something else will almost always include our own past. In this, we're still like the people on Dover Beach. But the uses of the past will be different. We stop asking for a moment whether there has been progress or degeneration, and we look at these two civilizations—say, Latin Christendom of five hundred years ago, and the West today—each as it stands on its own, with its greatness and misery, as though we had made a long voyage over the sea, rather than living in struggle through every wrenching year, on one side or the other of the battlefield, fortifications, or barricades.

I think that a better understanding emerges from this—better, that is, for our purposes, for Christians who want to know how to live in and with modernity. We liberate the present from the constriction of a too narrow comparison. Perhaps equally important, we also liberate the past. We escape the narrowness that I tried to designate (unfairly, I'm sure) with the term "a modern Catholicism," which sees itself as having freed itself from the crudities of the past and as having, at last, got it right. This is not because there aren't things in the past that I want to repudiate (the Inquisition, for starters) but because no period of Christian spirituality (and this goes beyond Christianity) can be reduced to its worst abuses, any more than modernity can be reduced to Auschwitz.

So the Ricci journey is meant to liberate the present from the dead hand of the polemics that its rise has generated, and it is meant similarly to liberate the past. This second effect is as important as the first because there is so much that we need in the past, so many spiritual forms, modes of prayer, devotion, of common life, that could help us revivify the love and service of God in the present. But they will help us only if we "lift from them the crushing weight of being *the* right answer," which somewhere got lost and whose existence condemns whatever came after (and also, needless to say, from the burden of being primeval error, which we have finally dispelled).

This is one of the things that excited me in Rosemary Luling Haughton's paper—for instance, her reference to the Neolithic cult of the goddess of birth and death and the relations we can find, or re-create, with the devotion to the Theotokos. The Catholic Church exists across all time; its orthodoxy, the rightness of its praise, consists of all the forms of devotion acceptable to God, somehow conjoined and resonating with each other. We stand somewhere in this web; our range is very limited. But those of us who come later have the great privilege that we can already begin this mutual resonation, retrieving some forms from the past, feeling the power of others, and charting our path in relation to them all.

So my imagined Ricci is also a time traveler. That is also a way of living our age, with its unparalleled knowledge of the past and even fascination with it. A Catholic way of living it, in the sense I'm using this term, would reject what Edward Thompson called "the enormous condescension of posterity" and allow the recognition to surface that, in God's eternity, we are contemporaries with the Neolithic tribespeople, and our prayers are heard by God together with theirs.

II

But I want to return to "transcendence" and to what I was trying to say with the term. There is a clear sense in which no term is going to do here because what I'm trying to say can't be said through one consistent formula. It demands to be expressed in two ways, which are complementary and also in tension.

One is the way I've foregrounded in the lecture. Take any conception of human flourishing, that makes no reference to something of intrinsic value beyond human flourishing, and we have something that is dangerously partial and incomplete, particularly because it cannot see that even things that negate this flourishing—solitary death, unremarked suffering, waning powers—can have the deepest human significance, just because they have more than human significance.

So here we speak of human flourishing and of something beyond it; we fall into a kind of dualism. We remember how this dualism has been used and abused, what has been done with oppositions like flesh-spirit, and material-spiritual.

We see, in particular, how much these oppositions have been wielded in a life-denying way, such as the "Catholic guilt and gloom about sex," and how this ends up making nonsense of the gospel—of John 10:10, for instance—and sliding Christian faith toward a kind of Stoicism, where the paradox of Christian renunciation disappears, and what is being let go is being affirmed in the very renunciation.

And so we want to turn to the other way of saying it, where the fullness of life is just following God, which is what the gospel means by "eternal life." We now have a monism. Human flourishing is not, in this way of putting it, "beyond life, though that life may reach beyond death."

But the last phrase alerts us to what is strange about this way of speaking. Life here takes us beyond death. In one way, this sounds (and, we believe, ultimately is) positive. As we live it, however, it means dying, undergoing death, coming to terms with something that on some level we cannot but experience as the denial of everything we value (an experience Jesus was not spared, in the garden and on the cross).

Here there is perhaps a nuance of difference between Rosemary

Luling Haughton and myself. She seems to want to see our affronting of death in the context of that "stiffening of heroism" our affirming of joy needs "because the achievement of justice . . . requires heroism as an ongoing way of life." That certainly makes sense applied to Jesus' acceptance of death, but death comes also to less heroic beings.

This perspective, in which the fullness of life means eternal life and death is taken in stride, is in an important sense the ultimately right one. It's important to hang on to this truth but impossible for many of us to live just in this perspective, or else we can do it only by bowdlerizing death and suffering (and thus also turning away from the gospel).

Rosemary Luling Haughton has the best word for our predicament here: bewildering. The best we can do is to tack back and forth between two languages, which on the surface look contradictory and which both can obscure central parts of the gospel. We try to avoid these pitfalls while recognizing that what we're trying to say evades our language; the formula that is ultimately truer is also further away from where we now live.

In my lecture, I put the dualistic formulation at the center because modern exclusive humanism does so. But we have to recognize how much a distorted Christian dualism helped to prepare the ground for this breach, and Rosemary Luling Haughton's discussion here does this, among other things.

III

I am very grateful to Jean Bethke Elshtain for her pages on Augustine, whose profound discussion of the links between the Trinity and the structure of the self give a fuller sense to the human being as *imago Dei*. Augustine's *de Trinitate* was the fruitful encounter of Trinitarian theology and the philosophical anthropology of his time.

This points to the possibility of a return engagement, in which the anthropology of our time can reconnect in its own way to the mystery of the Trinity. This must be already happening. I wish I knew the relevant literature, especially on the theological side.

We can see ways in which a philosophical anthropology is preparing the encounter. This may sound odd because the dominant philosophical stream of modern philosophy, descending from Descartes through Kant and on to today, is rigidly monological. But just because of this, there has been a reaction, and some facets of this have been immensely fruitful.

In calling the main modern tradition monological, I mean that it takes very little account of the fact that human beings are plural and even less account of their difference. This is not to say that either is denied, just that they don't seem to count for much in the constitution of the human powers that matter. So Descartes gives us a picture of an agent's building up a body of reliable knowledge entirely on his own, without leaning in any way on what others have learned, because to incorporate this, without putting it through the test of one's own monological recreation, would be to rely simply on authority.

Kant's ethical theory certainly takes account of human plurality because the most famous criterion for rightness involves the test of extending the maxim to everyone. But there is no place for difference; what is morally crucial about each one of us is precisely what we share with everyone else—indeed, what we would share with rational agents of any kind, even from beyond humanity.

So the human powers that are considered the most important in modernity, those of knowledge and ethical choice, have been conceived in a rigorously monological way. Of course, a lot of work has been done, "deconstructing" these positions. People have argued, for instance, that the full corpus of knowledge resides in no single head, that each of us has to take as given, on trust from multiple sources, a vast body of facts and lore and understandings, on the basis of which we can situate ourselves in the narrow realm where we really know what we're talking about.

Similarly, Kantian universalization, which for Kant was at the level of a kind of thought experiment (can you will this maxim as a universal law?), has been taken by Habermas into the realm of real exchange between people, where the telos is *de facto* general agreement, instead of just *de jure* universalization.

But, as one might expect, the hold of the monological view is a lot stronger than many critics think. They tinker with the surface rather than go to the deeper assumptions, which often lie so deep that they come across as just unchallengeable common sense.

Thus, Habermas demonologizes Kant, in the sense that an acceptable norm must now really be accepted by all those affected.

The aim is to do real justice to everyone, and so the goal is to bring everyone to the same point. But we still conceive of the people concerned as giving their agreement as individuals. The crucial issue is whether this fits with everyone's life plan, interest, needs, or desires.

There is obviously something important here. If the aim is to avoid oppression, injustice, and the control of some people by others, there is no surer bulwark in principle than this kind of requirement of universal unforced assent. The questionable assumption is that this procedure will not miss or even mangle some very important dimensions of human life.

And it does miss something important. We can get at this by saying that it is life in a certain kind of community, exemplified by families (where they are really working as such) and by friendships but also extending to larger-scale societies, of which churches are a prominent example. The crucial feature of these communities is that they live by goods that are discovered or made more fully evident or palpable within the community relationship. You don't really know what marital love is all about from outside this relationship, what friendship is before you've lived it, or as much about the love of God as a novice as you will long after your profession.

When you say something like this in some reaches of our liberal society, people jump all over you and ask whether you want to impose certain forms of community on people, to which the answer will very often be no. That misses the point, which is that we ought to be acknowledging a certain tension or dilemma in our moral and political lives. Individual assent is morally important and often indispensable. But if you think only of this, if you have as your only priority to protect the veto-exit option, then you impede the growth of community and the goods it can make accessible.

To put the point another way, we can ask, What does individual assent mean? Is it agreement by the individual in an identity quite independent of the community? Or by the individual who has come to live by the community goods? If the former, few communities would ever get started; if the latter, then the exit-veto option can't be everywhere equally appropriate.

Now in our present political world, it is perhaps good that public rules lean heavily toward protection of individual assent. But this is far from capturing all that is valuable in human life. To think that a rule like Habermas's exhausts morality is to be strangely blind to the human condition. Blind to what? To the place of those goods in human life that we can come to only together. And this blindness, which is rarely recognized as one possible view among others and instead seen as just common sense, comes from a much deeper and undeconstructed monologicality in modern thought. One could try to drag it out and express it in this way: it's as though the highest fulfillment in human life happens in the lives of individuals. By this I don't mean that people are blind to the need for collaboration and participation by others but, rather, that they think that the fulfillment itself happens in my mind, my feelings, my life. You may be instrumentally essential, and that is important, but the fulfillment is mine (and, of course, if the relation is reciprocal, you get it, too; this is not really an issue of selfishness in the ordinary sense). This being so, then, of course, I—even unaffiliated I—am the best judge of my good and always ought to exercise my right to assent.

What gets blocked out are what we might call essentially together-goods, where it is crucial to their being the goods they are that they be lived and enjoyed together, all the way from dance to conversation, to love, to friendship, to common self-rule, to the preaching of the Word. (One of the really illuminating turns in contemporary philosophy is Gadamer's reconstruction of our understanding of a conversation as a common action, more like a game or a dance than a series of causally linked monological actions.)

Further behind this assumption is a heroic picture of the human being, who ideally could be an epitome of human life singly, on his own (where the male pronoun is especially appropriate). It is as though the human nature we share were a full potentiality in each individual (like being a scientific genius, or a moral hero), and not something more like the potentiality to play our part in a certain kind of dance.

To break with this assumption is to see the fullness of human life as something that happens between people rather than within each one. So human nature is something that in principle—and not just *de facto*—cannot be conceived as existing in a single individual. This is the lesson Augustine seems to be drawing from the creation story, if I follow Jean Bethke Elshtain: out of one many, so that humans "be bound together not only by likeness of nature but also by a feeling of kinship."

The modern monological understanding culminates in the ideal of a society of like people—that is, a society bound together by what is essential to human beings, which is a nature similar in each one. In other words, they are bonded by "likeness of nature." What holds between them, ideally, is justice—that is, mutual respect for freedom and a fair distribution of chances to realize their humanity, each in his or her own life. What is hard to cope with in this picture is difference, except as something to be abstracted from. But what is feared and mistrusted is complementarity—that is, difference that is valued as a bond of mutual enrichment, the kind of thing that makes together-goods possible. This is central to a "feeling of kinship."

When you get to the point of seeing that what is important in human life is what passes between us, then you are coming close to the Trinity. It is not so surprising that the fullness of human life is what passes between humans, if the fullness of divine life passes between persons, and we are made in God's image. As a matter of fact, modern understandings of complementarity, which can be traced back through Humboldt to Herder, have in the latter's work an explicitly Christian source, even if not explicitly rooted in Trinitarian theology.

IV

I want to extend this discussion to add a further footnote to Jean Bethke Elshtain's very interesting paper. I have just said that the liberalism that arises from modern monological philosophy can't deal very well with difference. But there are also certain appeals to difference that are, in fact a refusal of exchange, of complementarity, which turn difference into incommensurability. These often present themselves as inspired by "postmodern" philosophy. But what is interesting about this many-stranded movement is that one feature it quite fails to "deconstruct" in the Western philosophical tradition is its monologicality.

Ironically, in this respect, much that flies under the banner of multiculturalism shares the crucial (and ultimately stultifying) assumptions of the procedural liberalism it likes to excoriate. In particular, they share with it either a commitment to negative liberty—that is, the voluntarist view of freedom—or/and a hostility to the Herder-Humboldt model of complementarity as the basis of the associative bond. Otherwise put, policies framed in the languages of postmodernism usually share these properties with their procedural liberal enemies.

There isn't room to argue this in detail. Let me take one example of a philosopher whose work is immensely influential in this field, Michel Foucault. Foucault was, in an important sense, a philosopher of freedom, in spite of his denials for a good part of his career; that is, he was a philosopher who claimed to unmask and lay bare domination, the interiorization of power relations by the victims, and although he often claimed that power had no subject, he certainly portrayed it as having victims. The moral thrust of these analyses, whether it was admitted or not in the text, was implicit in the language in which they were cast. They called for opening a line of resistance for the victim, a disengagement from the full grip of the current régime of power, particularly from its hold on our self-understanding. And Foucault's own interventions in politics and public life certainly bore out this interpretation.

Towards the end of his life, in the last volumes of the *History of Sexuality* and in the latest interviews, Foucault did make clearer his view of freedom, the building of an identity relatively uncolonized by the current régimes of power. And it was plainly a negative conception, as he makes quite unambiguous in the interview a number of us had with him in Berkeley a year before his death.[1]

A Foucaultian influence or at least an affinity with this position is evident in important strands of feminist theorizing, gay liberation, and some other calls for the recognition of "difference." The emphasis is on relations of oppression and on the undoing of these. The goal seems to be one in which the person or group concerned will have achieved full autonomy and will no longer be controlled or influenced. No place is allowed for another possible telos of this struggle, one in which the agents or the groups, previously related by modes of dominance, might reassociate on a better basis. The invocation of the victim scenario is a very common move in a position of this type. The history is usually painted in such a way as to make it almost inconceivable that there could be a new mode of association, let alone that both sides need it to be complete beings.

This brings me to the other facet I mentioned before, the rejection of the Herder-Humboldt complementarity view. In a sense, this, rather than the commitment to negative freedom, captures better the basic structure of Foucault's position. Foucault never paints the interpenetration of identities as a potential gain. He is, in this sense, the most profoundly anti-dialogical thinker. It is not that he puts forward an express thesis rejecting a dialogical view. It is rather that the stories he offers, at the different stages of his writings, of the development of identity always represent the definition of identity through the other in the register of invasive power, the preferred response to which must be resistance.

Thus, he discusses in *Surveiller et Punir* [2] the various modes of discipline that arise in the seventeenth and eighteenth centuries: parade square, asylum, prison—all forms of control. The development of modes of collective discipline by which people came to govern themselves—the modern reconstitution of civic freedom in puritan societies, for instance—all this remains completely outside his picture of our history. What Arendt defined as power, the increased capacity that people can create by associating in common action, remained completely off his map. He thought this kind of thing was an illusion, as he made quite clear in our interview in Berkeley.

On the contrary, what he defined as the only really healthy mode of identity formation, the definition of self in the aesthetic dimension,[3] was a completely solo operation, the achievement of lone virtuosi, who could learn from each other but didn't need to associate with each other. One could not be further removed from the Herder-Humboldt perspective.

But it is perhaps only in this perspective that one can distinguish destructive from creative modes of multi-culturalism. To put it oversimply, in judging different policies that fly under this title, the rule of thumb would be: What is the telos of the policy? Does it aim to restore a comity in which our need for each other can be met without the distortion of repression or exclusion? Or does the whole way in which the demand is framed point rather to liberation into solitary self-sufficiency as the only adequate solution? Worse still, does it point this way even if this liberation cannot, in fact, be reached, so that the protest is doomed to be repeated forever in a ritual of endless accusation?

V

I'd like to double back briefly and pick up a point made by Rosemary Luling Haughton. Our modern rights culture is a double-faced thing. I gave reasons for being celebratory about it, but it also is deeply rooted in a monological outlook. The very idea of expressing basic human norms in terms of rights already nudges us toward monologicality.

We can see this by looking at the peculiarities of the language of rights. As has often been pointed out, there is something rather special here. Many societies have held that it is good to ensure certain immunities or liberties to their members, or sometimes even to outsiders (think of the stringent laws of hospitality that hold in many traditional cultures). Everywhere it is wrong to take human life, at least under certain circumstances and for certain categories of persons. Wrong is the opposite of right, and so this is in some sense in play here.

But a quite different sense of the word is invoked when we start to use the definite or indefinite articles, or to put it in the plural and speak of "a right" or "rights" or when we start to attribute these to persons and speak of your rights or my rights. This is to introduce what has been called "subjective rights." Instead of saying that it is wrong to kill me, we begin to say that I have a right to life. The two formulations are not equivalent in all respects. In the latter case, the immunity or liberty is considered the property of someone. It is no longer just an element of the law that stands over and between all of us equally. That I have a right to life says more than that you shouldn't kill me. It gives me some control over this immunity. A right is something that in principle I can waive.[4] It is also something I have a role in enforcing.

Some element of subjective right exists perhaps in all legal systems. The peculiarity of the West was, first, that it played a bigger role in European medieval societies than elsewhere in history and, second, that it was the basis of the rewriting of natural law theory, which marked the seventeenth century. The older notion that human society stands under a law of nature, whose origin was the Creator and which was thus beyond human will, was now transposed. The fundamental law was reconceived as consisting of natural rights, attributed to individuals prior to society. At the origin of society stands a contract, which takes people out of a state of nature and puts them under political authority, as a result of an act of consent on their part.

So subjective rights are not just crucial to the Western tradition because they have been an important part of its jurisprudence since the Middle Ages. Even more significant is the fact that they were projected onto nature and formed the basis of a philosophical view of humans and their society, one that greatly privileges individuals' freedom and their right to consent to the arrangements under which they live. This view becomes an important strand in Western democratic theory of the last three centuries.

So, with all the benefits that have come from this language, we can see how it also is a standing invitation to constrict our thought into a monological mold. If we go all the way with this, then we are foursquare into the vision of a society of individuals bound together by justice, which we were discussing previously. The good of *solidarity*, in the sense Rosemary Luling Haughton uses this term, is neglected and devalued. In this sense, a "rights culture" and a "gospel ethic" are, indeed, far apart.

To complete the contemporary picture, we have to say that attempts are being made from within the rights language to correct for this narrowness, mainly by extending the schedule to new kinds of rights, such as collective rights, and rights to development. How successful these will be remains to be seen. But it is something to identify the problem here, a restriction built into our modern language, as Rosemary Luling Haughton has done.

VI

I'd like now to turn to the big question, raised by George Marsden in his paper, of the place of Christians in contemporary academic and intellectual life. This is the center of gravity of William M. Shea's tremendously interesting and informative paper, which fills out a big part of the picture of where we are now and how we got here.

A way into this vast subject could start from George Marsden's take on the image of a Ricci journey, which picked up on a facet that I wasn't thinking about: "Like Ricci dressing as a Confucian scholar, do we always have to dress our views in terms already acceptable to the contemporary academy?" Yes, we do a lot of that, obviously too much. The reasons are many, including not very admirable ones to do with the advantages (reputation, tenure, promotion) of conformity.

Underlying all that is the remarkable fact that academic culture in the Western world breathes an atmosphere of unbelief. I say remarkable fact because perhaps we aren't surprised enough by this phenomenon, which is a feature of this important subculture in our civilization rather than of the society in which it is set. It seems largely unaffected by differences between the societies. For instance, France, England, and the Scandinavian countries have a much lower level of religious belief and practice than the United States. A short walk through these societies convinces you of this fact. But their mainstream academic cultures (for these purposes, I'm setting aside confessional tertiary institutions) aren't all that different. Traveling from Birmingham, England, to Oakland, California (if I can invoke a well-known series of novels of our time), you notice the difference; traveling from the classrooms of the University of Birmingham to those of Berkeley, you could completely miss it.

Now the deeper historical reasons for this are hard to define, and I won't try here (although this is perhaps one of the most important intellectual tasks of our time). I want to talk about how it manifests itself. It's not just that there is a certain difficulty or embarrassment involved in introducing views that draw on some theistic basis or in avowing religious belief, though this is part of it. It is much more that unbelief has informed more than the answers; it has also shaped the questions. A young entrant into this world—say, an undergraduate or graduate student—might have strong faith, or be looking for ways of clarifying it through courses in history, politics, philosophy, or whatever. But in face of what is actually being discussed, it is often unclear how this relates to the student's agenda and even less clear how the things that are personally important could impinge on the discussion that is going on. There just seems to be no relevant place to make the kind of remarks that this student would like to make.

Add to this that beginning students are rarely too clear about what remarks they want to make anyway; we have more in the nature of confused intimations at that stage (indeed, we have a lot of those at this stage, too), and we can easily understand how a student slides into a pattern of conformity, which may then become a lifelong habit.

A striking example of this preshaped agenda is the aspect of moral theory, which I talked about in *Sources* and again in my lecture here. I argued in the lecture that a key issue for our times is that of moral sources, whether, for instance, we can maintain the high level of philanthropy and solidarity we now demand of ourselves, without these degenerating into their opposites: contempt, the need to control. The issue here is the quality of our moral motivation—in more old-fashioned terms, the quality of our will and the nature of the vision that sustains it.

Plato or Aristotle would have understood what I was talking about, although, of course, not the Christian and modern reference points of my discussion. But modern moral philosophy, particularly in the analytic world, has undergone a drastic foreshortening. These issues just fall off the agenda. For those thinking in the wake of the utilitarians and Kant, for instance, the principal moral question is, What ought we to do? (as against What is good to be? or What should we love?), and the principal task of moral philosophy is to find the principle or principles from which we can derive what we ought to do (the greatest happiness, or universalization, of whatever).

I was struck in some of the comments on *Sources* by how many people couldn't seem to grasp what question I was addressing. They took "moral sources" to be another name for the highest principles. They literally couldn't think outside the contemporary agenda.

But, one wants to protest, don't you see that it *also matters* whether people can actually bring themselves to *do* the right thing? But then your interlocutor looks at you blankly and says: of course, but that's not *moral philosophy*; how people actually get motivated, that's in the domain of psychology, or sociology, or whatever.

In other words, these two issues, what we should do and how we come to do it, which were unproblematically seen as part of the same inquiry by Plato, Augustine, and just about everybody else until the last three centuries, have been neatly sundered and placed in noncommunicating intellectual universes.

How did this strange divorce happen? There are lots of facets to the answer, including such crucial aspects of modernity as the affirmation of ordinary life and modern epistemology. But I want to bring out particularly the role of exclusive humanism itself in this transformation.

We can get a handle on what happened if we ask, Why were issues of the quality of the will central to, say, Plato?[5] It's clear that, for Plato, the very definition of justice requires that we identify a higher and a lower and distinguish our love of one from our love of the other. Christian faith could take this idea over while giving it a different content, and so Augustine speaks explicitly of "two loves." Recognition that there is a difference in us between higher and lower, straight and crooked, or loving and self-absorbed desires opens an intellectual space in which philosophy has a crucial role. I mean philosophy not in any narrow "disciplinary" definition but as the attempt to articulate and define the deepest and most general features of some subject matter—here, our moral being. This cannot just be handed over to some "empirical" science, unless this is carried out in a manner that incorporates this kind of reflection (which it is at its best in, say, Weber and Durkheim; I'm not making a statement about the property rights of disciplines).

Now this whole distinction between higher and lower fell under a deep cloud of suspicion in the eighteenth century and was expunged altogether in certain strands of the exclusive humanism that arises at this time. These are humanisms, as I said before, that see the good exclusively in terms of human flourishing, without any demand to give allegiance or worship to anything higher. The turn to these obviously also does away with an invocation of the higher in its earlier form. But interestingly, these first variants, which we can identify roughly with "Enlightenment humanism," retain a very strong agenda of universal justice and benevolence, inherited from Christianity and Stoicism.

Indeed, some variants do keep a conception of an imminentized higher motivation; they keep the distinction between lower and higher, but both terms are internal. Rousseau and Kant are evident examples. Here the issue of the quality of the will, What do you love? is obviously still an essential part of moral theory—even though with Kant it has already begun to be separated from the determination of what we ought to do.

But other streams were immensely influential. Two dominate the mainstream Enlightenment. I'm really going to invoke two ideal types here because most thinkers took something from each. These offer each its own way of casting the motivation to justice and benevolence as imminent, while they also bring about a revolution in relation to the earlier Christian and Stoic understandings of this motivation; the revolution consists in a rehabilitation of ordinary, untransformed human desire and self-love, previously seen as an obstacle to universal justice and benevolence, which now is cast either as innocent or as a positive force for good.

1. The "innocentizing" strategy paints human motivation as neutral; always a mode of self-love, it can be well or badly and irrationally or rationally directed. Guided by reason, it leads to justice and mutual aid. The extreme case, in which this ideal type is virtually unalloyed is, for example, Helvétius. Here the issue of the nature of our motivation disappears altogether. Everything depends on what guides it.

There is something here, analogous to the rise out of base, sensual self-absorption into a broader, higher, purer perspective, that figured in earlier views; this is the move from narrow, irrational, brutish, unenlightened ways of seeing the world to enlightenment and science. Science by its very nature involves our taking an objective and in this sense, universal perspective on things. To see human life in the view from nowhere or, to use a term of the epoch, from the standpoint of the "impartial spectator" is to think in universal and no longer parochial terms. But this rise is now coded as exclusively in the register of the understanding; the will remains constant.

Within this framework, it is clear why the quality of the will is irrelevant to ethics. What is needed to work out what we ought to do is purely disengaged reason.

2. The "positive" strategy is to paint original, unspoiled human motivation as including a bent toward solidarity with all others. The notion of sympathy was frequently invoked in this context in the eighteenth century. The extreme case of this ideal type can be seen in certain forms of primitivism: the noble savage has been corrupted, the original straight and healthy reactions have been overlaid. Rousseau in his primitivist moments reflects this (see the description of the unreflecting reactions of *pitié* in the original state of nature, in the second *Discourse*), although his full theory is much more complicated.

Some variants did lead to a two-quality view of the will, as we see with Rousseau, but in other cases the overlay was seen either in terms of error and superstition, in which case we return to natural solidarity through enlightenment (similar to strategy 1), or in terms of bad social arrangements, in which case we return to it through social engineering. In neither of these cases is the crucial change in the quality of will.

Here, as in case (1), there are important issues about how to bring about the right intention to justice and solidarity, but they involve quite different questions from that of determining what is right. Ethics doesn't have to concern itself with quality of will.

Now these eighteenth-century theories, in both variants, seem embarrassingly naive today. No one espouses them in these forms. The approach, however, lives on—for instance, in the highly therapeutic focus of much contemporary thought about good and bad, social and unsocial behavior. But the reality is vaguer and less intellectually satisfying. Much of our academic thinking takes place in a climate that has been set by the rise of exclusive humanism. It is not that people think explicitly about the issue of higher versus lower and then decide that it's not relevant to philosophical ethics. In spite of having read Plato in Ethics 101, this is almost never presented as a possible option today. Rather, the whole thing is just off the agenda, and the very attempt to raise it sounds undescribably quaint and dated, if not a little sinister.

And so the beginning student I invoked earlier doesn't know where to start or how to get a word in edgewise. The structure of the discussion (find the principle determining the right) might invite frontal attack: you just *oppose* God's command to any human criterion as the correct source. But for anyone who feels a connection to some form of Christian humanism, however balanced by a sense of the sovereignty of God, this can't do justice to the position. You can get at what's wrong with what you're being taught only if you can open up all the closed and neglected corridors in the ethical mansion.

All this leads me to believe that the most important thing Christian scholars should attempt is to change the agenda, open it up. This may mean bringing back issues that may not immediately, on their face, relate to Christian faith—like this question of the place of the quality of the will in moral philosophy. We have to think of the ways in which our whole debate with modernity, our friendly yet adversarial exchange, is impeded and stifled by a drastically foreshortened intellectual agenda and then move to widen this. If we can get to the point where mainstream people have to *defend* the narrow focus, we will have succeeded.

VII

Of course, this won't be easy, not just because of the great intellectual difficulties but because there is a lot of hostility out there.

There is in modern humanism an element of "anti-Christian rebellion." The debates we want to open arouse a lot of anger on both sides. I want to conclude with a few remarks about the place of anger.

When I hear an exclusivist humanism waxing indignant about the crimes and errors of the church in history, I often partly agree. We all feel this today at some point; who defends the Inquisition? My feelings are divided, complex. But I also see a complexity in my interlocutor, who has an important moral point but is also resisting something: resisting the insight that the love of God is something bigger and more important and more powerful than all this human bumbling and evil.

But then that makes us brothers under the skin. We all—believers and unbelievers alike—spend a lot of energy resisting God. It takes a lifetime of prayer to melt the resistances, and even then. . . . And one thing we can immediately see, from our own case as well, is that anger, righteous anger, is a great weapon of resistance. Our modern Western world is awash in righteous anger, reciting litanies of abuse and obloquy. The point is often well taken, in that the abuses are or have been real and crying.

Beyond this, what the anger is often doing for people is stopping their moral and spiritual growth because it's a tremendously effective resistance against it. For one thing, I feel good about myself because, whatever my minor imperfections, they pale into insignificance in face of the horrible deeds of those (communists or capitalists, white males or feminists, etc.). For another, I certainly don't need to bother about any insights I might gain from those unspeakable enemies of humanity, God, or whatever.

We have to be more aware of what anger is doing for us, as resisters—and therefore against us, as lovers of God. That is what makes me so chary of the often snarling tone adopted by much of the Christian Right in the present U.S. culture wars. Of course, anti-Christian attack can be provoking. I have to admit my practice falls far below that suggested by my serene tone here. When it is suggested that, by virtue of my being a Catholic, I must be working night and day for the return of the Inquisition, I usually fly into a rage and throw back some (I hope) stinging rebuke.

Occasionally, I laugh. The whole scene, like all the modalities of human superrighteousness, has its richly comic side. And then I am tempted to say, in the words that open the choral part of

Beethoven's Ninth Symphony, "Come off it. Let's both calm down and listen to each other." Changing the tone might be the essential prelude to changing the content.

Notes

1. "Politics and Ethics: An Interview," in Paul Rabinow, ed., *The Foucault Reader* (New York: Pantheon, 1984), 373–380.

2. Michel Foucault. *Surveiller et Punir* (Paris: Gallimard, 1976).

3. See Hubert Dreyfus and Paul Rabinow, *Michel Foucault: Beyond Structuralism and Hermeneutics,* 2nd ed. (Chicago: University of Chicago Press, 1983), 237, 251.

4. Which is why Locke had to introduce a restrictive adjective to block this option of waiver when he spoke of "inalienable rights." The notion of inalienability had no place in earlier natural right discourse because this had no option of waiver.

5. Of course, I am using an expression, "quality of the will," which is outrageously anachronistic in connection with Plato, but I believe it can be easily translated into the local dialect. For Plato, the issue was, What do you love (*philein*)?

Index

CPSIA information can be obtained at www.ICGtesting.com
Printed in the USA
BVOW03*0401030215

385867BV00003B/9/P